EMP

SURVIVAL:

How to Prepare Now and Survive When an Electromagnetic Pulse Destroys Our Power Grid

Larry and Cheryl Poole

Dedication

Dedicated to our children and grandchildren
and to those of our readers.
May they read, prepare, live confidently and survive.

Acknowledgements

We wish to thank the scientists and political leaders who have presented evidence of the EMP threat in numerous hearings since 1997. Some day in the future, we hope their concerns will be recognized and the nation will be protected.

The nation should thank the following leaders who have testified at congressional hearings about the EMP threat.

Dr. Lowell L. Wood, Jr,

Dr. William R. Graham,

Dr. Peter Vincent Pry,

U.S. Representative Roscoe Bartlett,

Dr. Gary L. Smith,

U.S. Senator John Kyl,

U.S. Representative Yvette D. Clarke,

U.S. Representative Curt Weldon, and

Dr. Michael J. Frankel,

We also want to acknowledge all the members of the EMP Commission that produced the "Report of the Commission to Assess the Threat to the United States from Electromagnetic Pulse (EMP) Attack",

Dr. John S. Foster, Jr.,

Mr. Earl Gjelde,

Dr. William R. Graham, Chair,

Dr. Robert J. Herrmann,

Mr. Henry M. Kluepfel,

Gen. Richard L. Lawson, USAF retired,

Dr. Gordon K. Soper,

Dr. Lowell L. Wood Jr.,

Dr. Joan B. Woodard

The bipartisan EMP Commission was established in 2001 and re-commissioned again in 2006 to examine potential threats, vulnerabilities of the U.S. military and civilian infrastructures and recommend measures to counter EMP threats. The EMP Commission has expired.

Military strategists in four countries have boasted about their ability to cripple the U.S.

A low cost, short range missile from an ocean freighter launched 12 miles off the U.S. coast could achieve an EMP effect.

Our power grid is not protected. A widespread power outage could last months or years.

We wrote this book after reading Congressional testimony about the EMP (electromagnetic pulse) threat in hearings from 1997 to 2010. Our nation continues to be vulnerable. It will be up to the individual American family to survive.

Table of Contents

Boxed Text excerpts throughout the book are from the 2008 "Critical National Infrastructure" report of the Commission to Assess the Threat to the United States from Electromagnetic Pulse (EMP)

Disclaimer

This book is believed to contain correct information based on our personal research and preparation. We do not make any warranty, express or implied or assume any legal responsibility for the accuracy, completeness, or usefulness of any information product or process disclosed or represent that its use would not infringe on privately owned rights. Reference to any specific commercial product process or service by its trade name or manufacturer or otherwise, does not necessarily constitute or imply its endorsement, recommendation or favoring by the authors. The information in the book should not be a substitute for professional advice and training. The authors disclaim any responsibility for problems that may occur by following the information in this text.

Prelude

In an instant, everything could change. We would no longer be a superpower, but a pre-industrial nation. Mass hunger, mob violence, and rampant diseases could change our way of life for decades.

PART ONE
EMP
(Electromagnetic Pulse)

Chapter One
EMP (Electromagnetic Pulse) Basics

There will be no sound and no warning. In an instant, cars will stop, computers and radios will shut down and electronic devices will cease to function. Many devices will be permanently damaged, their wires and circuits "fried". In our utility industries, the electric power grids, telecommunication networks, public water systems, public sewer treatment, transportation systems, and emergency services could suffer irreparable damage.

Dependent on the nature of the damage, the exposure of the electronics, or the height of the detonation, the electricity may come back in a few hours, or years.

Repairs could take days or years, depending on the ability of crews to measure the damage without electronics and obtain the replacement parts, no longer made in the U.S. If the electricity is off for more than a year, the loss of life would run into the tens of millions. [1]

Four nations now boast that they have developed an EMP weapon that they plan to use to attack the U.S. It is not surprising, 128,000 nuclear warheads have been built since 1945 and many are not accounted for. Over 10,000 missiles owned by 30 countries are capable of lifting a nuclear weapon over the U.S. [2] There are about 35,000 Scud ballistic missiles at the present time. Scud missiles can be purchased for $100,000 by anyone. [3] Terrorist organizations own ocean freighters. Enemies potentially have the weapons, the launchers and the vehicles to launch an attack just miles off the U.S. coast.

How was EMP discovered?

Enrico Fermi, the brilliant WWII Manhattan Project physicist, predicted that a nuclear explosion would generate strong electromagnetic fields over a large area.

In 1962, during atmospheric testing of a small nuclear device, U.S. scientists were surprised by the electromagnetic pulse affect over a few million square miles in the mid-Pacific. Radio stations were shut down, cars stopped, phone systems were burned out, traffic lights turned off nearly 1000 miles away from the blast.[4]

---

[1] Dr. Wood, Lowell, testimony, *"Terrorism and the EMP Threat to Homeland Security"*, U.S. Senate, Committee on the Judiciary, Subcommittee on Terrorism, Technology and Homeland Security, testimony, March 8, 2005, p 18

[2] Major Miller, Colin R., USAF, *"Electromagnetic Pulse Threats in 2010"*, Maxwell AFB, Air War College, Center for Strategy and Technology, November 2005, p 390

[3] Dr. Wood, Lowell, *"Terrorism and the EMP Threat to Homeland Security"*, Subcommittee on Terrorism, Technology, and Homeland Security, Committee on the Judiciary, March 8, 2005, p 11

[4] Dr. Wood, Lowell testimony, "Threat *Posed by Electromagnetic Pulse (EMP) to U.S. Military Systems and Infrastructure"*, U.S. House of Representatives, Military Research and Development Subcommittee, Committee on National Security, July 16, 1997 p 34

The Soviets were reportedly surprised at the 600 km (373 miles) range of electrical damage in overhead and underground cables from an EMP after a nuclear test in 1962.[5] Surge arrestors burned out, fuses blew and power supplies broke down in each of three tests. The three test detonations were at heights of 60km, 150 km and 300km.[6] (37, 93 and 186 miles)

Both of the countries experienced damage worse than expected. The extent of the damage is because an EMP can travel through metallic conductors, railroad tracks, power lines, and communication lines.

What is an EMP?

The EMP is used as a strategic weapon by inducing damaging voltages and currents that electrical circuits are not designed to withstand. EMP's are lethal to electronic systems. The smaller and more sophisticated electronics are especially prone to damage.

Nuclear EMP weapons detonated at high altitude can span continents. The EMP weapons affect electronics at least within the line of sight of the detonation. The higher the altitude at detonation, the wider the impact. The EMP attacks can reach a radius of 1500 miles, causing widespread electronic destruction.

Dr. Lowell Wood, a leading EMP researcher and member of the EMP Commission described the following about the nature of EMP in his statement to the U.S. House,

---

[5] Dr. Foster, John, S, Jr, Earl Gjelde, Dr. William R Graham, et al, "Executive Report", Report of the Commission to Assess the Threat to the United States from Electromagnetic Attack, 2004 p 4

[6] Ibid

Armed Services Committee in 1999. The following is a brief summary based on his prepared statement.[7]

1. EMP is really severe static electricity, everywhere all at once- since the damage occurs thousands of times more swiftly than a lightning strike, the lightning protective devices are essentially useless

2. EMP can blanket an entire U.S.-sized continent from a single source. It originates from the interaction of gamma radiation from a nuclear explosion with the Earth's atmosphere.

3. EMP doesn't linger. It lasts for milliseconds.

4. EMP isn't sensed by people and doesn't damage the human body.

5. EMP is more threatening to big electrical systems than to small ones –physically large systems comprised of metal lines, cables, wire and dish antennae often manifest great vulnerability to EMP damage

6. EMP is much more threatening to modern electronics than to old-fashioned ones. The shrinking size of electronic parts increases their vulnerability.

7. EMP affects in space, is different and more damaging.

8. EMP defenses are simple. Hardening may consist of metallic shielding of a tinfoil like covering.

---

[7] Dr. Lowell Wood, "Prepared Statement" "*Electromagnetic Pulse Threats to U.S. Military and Civilian Infrastructure*", Committee on Armed Services, Subcommittee Military Research and Development, U.S. House, October 7, 1999

How would an EMP weapon be launched?

Some scientists claim that terrorists lack the expertise to carry out an EMP attack. A scud launcher with a crude nuclear weapon on a tramp steamer operated by a terrorist group is all that is necessary.[8] They don't have to be technical geniuses. If they miss by 100 miles, it doesn't matter.[9] The missile does not have to strike a specific target, only to detonate a weapon at least 40 km (25 miles) in height to create an EMP. The U.S. early warning satellites and radar systems may not have enough time to react to a missile launched from a ship.

A missile deployed on an ocean freighter could create an EMP that covers all of the East coast or the West Coast and create a disaster several times over in magnitude of Hurricane Katrina.[10]

In addition to the widespread nuclear EMP attacks, non-nuclear EMP technologies are now proliferating in terrorist groups and rogue nations. These smaller EMP weapons are capable of damaging electronics in a mile radius. These smaller weapons of limited range will cause chaos, but will not cause the catastrophic loss of power described in this book.

The survival plans described in this book is for a widespread EMP event. It could be caused by a first-

---

[8] Rep. Bartlett, Roscoe, Testimony, *"Threat Posed By Electromagnetic Pulse Attack"*, Committee on Armed Services, U.S. House of Representatives, Washington DC, July 10, 2008 p 10

[9] Rep. Bartlett, Roscoe, Testimony, *"Threat Posed By Electromagnetic Pulse Attack"*, Committee on Armed Services, U.S. House of Representatives, Washington DC, July 10, 2008 p 10

[10] Dr. Graham, William, Testimony, *"Threat Posed by Electromagnetic Pulse Attack,"*, U.S. House, Committee on Armed Services, July 10, 2008 p 11

generation nuclear weapon. Any nuclear weapon, even a low yield one, could cause a catastrophic EMP event.

The height of the detonation would determine the extent of the EMP affect.

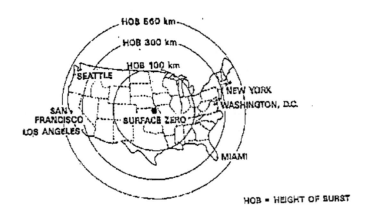

11

At 100 km height, (62 miles), about half of the continental U.S., would be affected. The diagram displays the range if detonated in the center of the country. Most scientists expect detonations near the coasts.

A detonation at an altitude of 250 miles could produce a 10-50 kilovolt/meter (kV/m) electrical pulse, enough to produce extensive damage to electronics over the entire continent[12]. Our electronics are vulnerable, a pulse of just 10kV/m causes electrical charges a billion times more powerful than some systems were designed to tolerate.[13]

---

[11] Dr. Smith, Gary L. Statement, *"Threat Posed by an Electromagnetic Pulse to U.S. Military Systems and Civilian Infrastructure"*, Subcommittee on Military Research and Development, Figure 2, Extent of HEMP Coverage, July 16, 1997

[12] Major Miller, Colin R., *"Electromagnetic Pulse Threats in 2010"*, Center for Strategy and Technology Air War College, Air University, Maxwell AFB, AL, November 2005, p 389

[13] Major Miller, Colin R., *"Electromagnetic Pulse Threats in 2010"*, Center for Strategy and Technology Air War College, Air University, Maxwell AFB, AL, November 2005, p 388

The pulse occurs too quickly to take emergency action to stop the destruction.

In some cases the pulse actually melts critical components.[14] Wires in computer chips can be permanently damaged by a few tenths of an amp.[15]

An EMP with a field level of 100kV/m can damage even unplugged electronics.

The electromagnetic pulse travels through wires, pipes and antenna and can travel across power grids, destroying electronics as it passes in less than a second.

The extent of the damage could cascade into 70% of the nation's power grid. It is one of many vulnerabilities of our power grid that is known, but with little response from industry or the government.

How does an electromagnetic pulse (EMP) cause damage?

There are three stages in the EMP, each with its own lethality to electronics.

The three stages are labeled E1, E2 and E3. [16] E1 occurs in nanoseconds and will affect electronics, communications, protective systems, generators, and fuel systems. It can be easily prevented through shielding.

The E2 is like lightning but more widespread. It resembles a thousand to a million lightning strikes.

---

[14] Major Miller, Colin R., "*Electromagnetic Pulse Threats in 2010*", Center for Strategy and Technology Air War College, Air University, Maxwell AFB, AL, November 2005, p 388

[15] Major Miller, Colin R., "*Electromagnetic Pulse Threats in 2010*", November 2005 p 388

[16] Dr. Foster, John, S, Jr, Earl Gjelde, Dr. William R Graham, et al, "*Critical National Infrastructures*", Report of the Commission to Assess the Threat to the United States from Electromagnetic Attack, April 2008 p 34-35

E3 will last a minute or longer. The E3 damage can also be caused by a solar storm. E3 flows through electricity transmission lines, damaging transmitters and power lines. Every EMP attack has all three stages delivered in sequence and almost spontaneously.

The serious threat of solar storms will be discussed later.

Is it safe to discuss the details of an EMP attack openly?

The EMP Commission considered the same question. When they reviewed the literature, they found extensive knowledge of EMP and its effects throughout the world. Dr. William R. Graham, the Chairman of the EMP Commission, testified about the asymmetric situation, "..in our survey of potentially hostile countries, they talk about this (EMP) extensively in the open literature, and did before the commission was even established."[17] Our enemies know more about EMP than Americans.

Why don't Americans know about EMP?

When the U.S. began nuclear testing no mention was made to the public about the potential to affect electronics. When the scientific community saw the potential offensive uses of EMP, release of information was further limited. Few articles appeared in open literature for decades.

While the U.S. was guarding the discovery, the Soviets were training their military and civilian population, building protective hardware for their vulnerable systems

---

[17] Dr. Graham, William, Testimony, "*Threat Posed by Electromagnetic Pulse Attack*", July 10, 2008 p 11

and developing enhanced EMP weapons. During this time the U.S. became the most vulnerable and the least protected country.

In recent years, EMP information has still not been openly discussed. Dr. Graham was asked about the lack of interest during testimony. He replied, "It might be better to ask a sociologist than an engineer and physicist that question. But it falls into the category of a problem which hasn't happened yet. ..But it is just not within our character and our society to look for these events before they occur."[18]

In the U.S., unlike our enemies, EMP was considered a serious but unlikely possibility. While other militaries invested and reportedly developed a new generation of super-EMP's, the U.S. government and power industry has chosen not even to invest in EMP protection.

EMP weapons are still not considered weapons of mass destruction (WMD). However, it is recognized by scientists that the secondary humanitarian crisis created by a large scale EMP attack will cause massive mortality.

What foreign countries present an EMP threat to the U.S.?

Foreign militaries are more confident that the U.S. will be attacked with an EMP, than our government is.

Dr. Lowell Wood stated that the Soviets decided years ago, that EMP represented an exceptionally severe threat but also offered the Soviets extraordinary opportunities as a weapon. The Soviets deployed protective hardware,

---

[18] Dr. Graham, William, testimony, " *Threat Posed by Electromagnetic Pulse Attack*",, U.S. House Armed Services Committee, July 10, 2008, p11

"hardening", lavishly in their home country. They have a strong respect for the EMP impact and use as a weapon. The Russians have not retired their EMP strike ability.

In testimony to the U. S. Senate Homeland Security Subcommittee, Dr. Peter Vincent Pry, said that Russian and Chinese military scientists describe in public writings their intent to use weapons in order to achieve an EMP effect to destroy U.S. military and civilian electronic systems. They report their super-EMP's can destroy even the best protected U.S civilian electronic system.[19]

Dr. Graham testified that two senior Russian generals admitted that the Russians had developed what they called the super-EMP weapon that could generate fields in the range of 200 kilovolts/meter. [20] According to testimony, protective hardening against EMP of missiles and communication systems in the U.S. were designed during the Cold War to protect critical equipment up to 50kV/m.[21] The new Super-EMP weapons produce four times the field that our critical systems were protected against.

The Russian generals stated some engineers were working privately with North Korea in the design of nuclear weapons.[22]

North Korea is reportedly working on an EMP bomb that if exploded 25 miles above the earth could damage

[19] Dr Pry, Peter Vincent , statement," *Terrorism and the EMP Threat to Homeland Security*", U.S. Senate, Subcommittee on Terrorism, Technology and Homeland Security, March 8, 2005, p 7

[20] Dr. Graham, William, *"Threat Posed by Electromagnetic Pulse Attack,"*, Committee on Armed Services, July 10, 2008 p 9

[21] Dr. Graham, William, *"Threat Posed by Electromagnetic Pulse Attack,"*, Committee on Armed Services, July 10, 2008 p 9

[22] Dr. Graham, William, *"Threat Posed by Electromagnetic Pulse Attack"*,, U.S. House Armed Services Committee July 10, 2008, p 9

electronics within 450 miles. Newspapers and websites reported recently that in defense against an attack, South Korea was working on an $80 million EMP defense system.

In testimony in 2005, describing North Korea's missile range limits, Dr. Peter Vincent Pry, said "Today, North Korea is reportedly on the verge of achieving an ICBM capability with its Taepo-Dong-2 missile, estimated to be capable of delivering a nuclear weapon to the U.S."[23]

Dr. Wood reinforced in testimony that North Korea "potentially has the most advanced nuclear weapons that exist on the planet because they have received a great deal of foreign assistance."[24]

Iran's rocket tests have detonated at high altitude, exactly the strategy for a high altitude EMP attack. The western press described the tests as "failures" because they didn't hit a target; however, Iran describes them as "successful". The tests were "successful" if Iran was practicing for an EMP attack.[25] The goal of an EMP attack would be to detonate at the highest altitude to cause the greatest damage. Further evidence is that Iran is known to have launched a Scud missile from a vehicle in the Caspian Sea[26], a method which could support the expectation of an attack on the U.S. from off shore.

Dr. Pry testified that an Iranian political-military journal article entitled "Electronics to Determine Fate of Future

[23] Dr. Pry, Peter Vincent *"Terrorism and the EMP Threat to Homeland Security"*, U.S. Senate Subcommittee on Terrorism, Technology and Homeland Security, Committee on the Judiciary, March 8, 2005, p 10

[24] Dr. Wood, Lowell, *"Terrorism and the EMP Threat to Homeland Security"*, U.S. Senate Subcommittee, p17

[25] Dr. Pry, Peter Vincent, *"Terrorism and the EMP Threat"* March 8, 2005, p 9

[26] Dr. Pry, Peter Vincent, *"Terrorism and the EMP Threat"*, U.S. Senate Subcommittee, March 8, 2005, p 11

Wars" states that the key to defeating the U.S. is EMP attack.[27]

Dr. Pry testified to a Senate Subcommittee on Terrorism about the Chinese military perspective, "Chinese military writings are replete with references to the dependency of United States military forces and civilian infrastructure upon sophisticated electronic systems and to the potential vulnerability of those systems."[28]

Dr. Pry continued his testimony about China, describing a quote from an official Chinese newspaper, "…When a country grows increasingly powerful economically and technologically, it will become increasingly dependent on modern information systems. The United States is more vulnerable to attacks than any other country in the world."[29]

While we remain vulnerable, other governments are protecting their infrastructure. Dr. Pry testified "Numerous foreign governments have invested in hardening programs to provide some protection against nuclear EMP attack, indicating that this threat has broad international credibility."[30]

The EMP attack may create less stigma for the attacker. Dr. Pry revealed in his testimony, "Some foreign analysts, judging from open source statements and writings, appear

---

[27] Dr. Pry, Peter Vincent, *"Terrorism and the EMP Threat"* U.S. Senate Subcommittee, , March 8, 2005, p 8

[28] Dr. Pry, Peter Vincent, *"Terrorism and the EMP Threat to Homeland Security"*, Subcommittee on Terrorism, Technology, and Homeland Security, Committee on the Judiciary, March 8 2005, p 7

[29] Dr. Pry, Peter Vincent, *"Terrorism and the EMP Threat to Homeland Security"*, Subcommittee on Terrorism, Technology, and Homeland Security, Committee on the Judiciary, March 8 2005 p 8

[30] Dr. Pry, Peter Vincent, *"Terrorism and the EMP Threat to Homeland Security"*, Subcommittee on Terrorism, Technology and Homeland Security, Committee on the Judiciary, March 8 2005 p5

to regard EMP attack as a legitimate use of nuclear weapons because EMP would inflict no or few prompt civilian casualties."[31]

Is our military prepared for an EMP attack?

The U.S. military has begun investing in hardware protection for its own equipment against EMP attack. In 2008 testimony, Dr. Graham describes the Department of Defense as in the "planning stage" of EMP hardening.[32]

In March 2010, the U.S. Navy resurrected their EMP team that had been inactive for ten years.[33] The probability of EMP attack increases each year as new weapons are developed and EMP construction is even detailed in open writings. Our military may be more likely to survive the attack undamaged than the civilian population due to some hardening. However, the armed forces rely on a great amount of power from the national grid, which is very vulnerable.

Any long-range missile attacks will be defended by the U.S. ground-based missile defense systems. However, there is a movement by powerful leaders in our government to reduce these missile defense systems.

The defense of potential attacks by Scuds or Shahab-3 missiles that could be fired from a ship near our coastline requires a different strategy. Al Qaeda is known to own 80 freighters.[34]

---

[31] Dr. Pry, Peter Vincent, *"Terrorism and the EMP Threat"*, March 8 2005, p 6

[32] Dr. Graham, William, Dr. Graham, William, *"Threat Posed by Electromagnetic Pulse Attack,"*, Committee on Armed Services, July 10, 2008 p 12

[33] EMPact America, *"Frequently asked Questions"*, http://www.empactamerica.org/faq.php printed 10/27/2010

Scientists believe the freighter-based trajectory would not allow enough time for defense. The U.S. fleet of Aegis ships, some with interceptor missiles, can monitor attackers through radar if they are in position.

What equipment and components are vulnerable to EMP?

The EMP will cause permanent damage in some equipment. EMP stresses can significantly exceed ordinary stresses on electrical circuits and components.

Antenna-like conductors will bring the EMP into a computer, radio, or any electrical device. Wires, circuits, and pipes are attractive to an EMP. An EMP producing at least 100 kilovolts/meter (kV/m) would damage any device with a lot of wires inside.[35] The damage might occur even if it was not plugged in.

Typical surge protectors probably won't protect against an EMP because of the exceptional "rise time" in nanoseconds.[36]

Satellites in low earth orbit would be lost within a week due to radiation in the atmosphere, or immediately because of the ground station loss.[37]

The EMP Commission tested fifty cars for EMP effect at 25kV/m. 10% stopped running. One or two had to have

[34] Dr. Pry, Peter Vincent, *"Terrorism and the EMP Threat to Homeland Security"*, Subcommittee on Terrorism, Technology and Homeland Security, Committee on the Judiciary, March 8 2005 p 22

[35] Dr. Graham, William, testimony, *"Threat Posed by Electromagnetic Pulse Attack,"*, U.S. House, Committee on Armed Services, July 10, 2008, p 28

[36] Rep. Bartlett, Roscoe, "Threat *Posed by Electromagnetic Pulse Attack,"*, U.S. House, Committee on Armed Services, July 10, 2008, p 27

[37] Dr. Graham, William, *"Threat Posed by Electromagnetic Pulse Attack,"*, U.S. House, Committee on Armed Services, July 10, 2008 p 27

the computer chip replaced to restart. [38] There would be more damage expected at a higher level EMP.

Dr. Graham testified about the impact on cars at a higher level, "… certainly 100 kilovolts/meter and possibly to 50 kilovolts per meter, you would have quite a few more failures."[39]

Airplanes are not hardened against EMP. They are tested for lightning strikes, so they have some level of electromagnetic protection. However, EMP contains some electromagnetic frequencies not present in lightning. The potential pulse of an EMP is far greater than a lightning strike. Because of the software and electronics some aircraft will probably be lost.

The most critical equipment in the power grid in an EMP are the major transformers. The transformers will burn out and they may not be repairable. Replacements are built overseas, and there is no extra inventory available. Even in normal circumstances, it takes one to two years to replace one. If the U.S. suddenly needed hundreds of transformers, it could take decades.[40] The next chapter explores the power industry and EMP effects.

What about the EMP risk of a solar storm?

[38] Dr. Graham, William, *"Threat Posed by Electromagnetic Pulse Attack,"*, U.S. House, Committee on Armed Services, July 10, 2008 p 22

[39] Graham, William, *"Threat Posed by Electromagnetic Pulse Attack,"*, U.S. House, Committee on Armed Services, July 10, 2008, p 26

[40] Dr. Wood, Lowell, testimony, *"Terrorism and the EMP Threat to Homeland Security"*, U.S. Senate Subcommittee on Terrorism, Technology, and Homeland Security, Committee on the Judiciary,, p 20

The EMP Commission acknowledged the solar storm potential, "The commission recognized that EMP is one of several threats to the overall electrical power system. Some of these threats are naturally occurring such as geomagnetic storms."[41]

A significant solar storm can produce nearly the same effect as an intentional EMP attack. The U.S. is more vulnerable than other nations to a solar storm because of our reliance on sophisticated electronic systems.

The sun is currently cycling into a solar maximum period of solar flares and coronal mass ejections. Great magnetic storms occur about every century. They have not occurred since the development of, and our reliance on, the electric power grid. We have never been so vulnerable to a solar storm.

Dr. Yousaf M. Butt, a space scientist who wrote about EMP in *Space Review* is concerned about the power system collapse from a geomagnetic solar storm. However, he does not think an EMP attack is likely, because he reasons, the lack of technical expertise by terrorists and the political sensibilities of nations. He says, "However, it is virtually guaranteed that a powerful geomagnetic storm, capable of knocking out a significant section of the US electrical grid, will occur within the next few decades."[42]

The geomagnetic storms, he says, have a potential to cause long-term power grid blackouts, unprecedented transformer damage, lengthy restoration times and

---

[41] Dr. Foster, John S. Jr. Earl E. Gjelde, William R Graham et al, *"Critical National Infrastructures"*, Report of the Commission to Assess the Threat to the United States from Electromagnetic Pulse Attack, July 10, 2008, p 18

[42] Dr. Butt, Yousaf M, *"The EMP Threat: fact, fiction, and response"*, February 1, 2010, The Space Review, http://www.thespacereview.com/article/1553/1

chronic shortages for multiple years.[43] These are the same effects expected from an EMP attack.

In 1859, a powerful solar storm called the "Carrington Event", burned telegraph wires across Europe and America. A similar storm today could create effects similar to an EMP attack.

The National Academies of Sciences predicted in a 2008 report that a solar geomagnetic storm as severe as the Carrington event could inflict $1-2 trillion dollars and take 4-10 years to recover.[44]

A geomagnetic storm in Quebec in 1989 caused a nine hour blackout on 6 million people and caused $10 million in damage to the power company and tens of millions in damage to their customers.[45]

The National Oceanic and Atmospheric Administration issued an advisory on August 14, 2010 of the first solar radiation storm in years, partially directed toward Earth. This was the same day the U.S. Senate Energy Committee removed electromagnetic grid protections from their version of an energy bill.

What protections are there for the civilian infrastructure?

[43] Dr. Butt, Yousaf M, "*The EMP threat: fact, fiction and response*", The Space Review, February 1, 2010 from www.thespacereview.com/article/1553/1

[44] Dr. Philips, Tony, *Severe Space Weather, Social and Economic Impacts*, January 21, 2009, science@NASA, referencing Space Studies Board, National Academy of Sciences, , "*Severe Space Weather Events-Understanding Societal and Economic Impacts*", National Academies Press, Washington DC 2008

[45] Ibid

The EMP protection in the civilian infrastructure is non-existent. Our civilian telephone, electricity, broadband communications and electronics plants are all vulnerable to nuclear-armed enemies.

In a statement to the Armed Services Committee in 1999, Dr. Lowell Wood stated "It obviously makes no sense to gain an EMP-robust military machine while the National civilian electrical/electronic infrastructure remains tissue-soft."[46] More than a decade later, the situation is unchanged.

In 2005, Dr. Wood testified to the U.S. Senate subcommittee about the civilian infrastructure, he reported that we are exceedingly vulnerable and that could entice an attack.[47]

There are currently no incentives for EMP protection investments by the power industry, nor penalties for failing to prepare.

There are no regulations enforced by the government on the patchwork of independent, but interconnected, public, private and cooperative electric power companies.

The interconnected design of our power grid and communication networks will allow the EMP to propagate across power grid regions. Our power industry equipment and electronic devices are susceptible to an EMP attack because they are not built with protective shielding.

Even the large transformers, no longer built in the U.S., and critical to the power system, are not protected.

[46] Wood, Dr. Lowell, "Statement", Armed Services Committee, U.S. House
http://armedservices.house.gov/comdocs/testimony/106thcongress/99-10-07wood.htm

[47] Dr. Wood, Lowell "*Terrorism and the EMP Threat to Homeland Security*", March 8, 2005, p 31

Is the Department of Homeland Security (DHS) focused on the EMP threat?

Since the EMP threat was first presented to Congress in 1997, there has been a reluctance to commit resources to protect the country. The frustration and impatience of scientists who have spent decades studying the EMP potential are evident in our reading of their testimonies in 1997, 1999, 2004, 2008 and 2010 hearings.

In August 2010, Dr. Michael J. Frankel, a physicist and executive director of the EMP Commission testified to the Senate Subcommittee on Terrorism and Homeland Security. He said there has been "no detectable resonance as yet out of the DHS,"[48] and that, "as a result the Commission's recommendations seem to have simply languished". He added, "along with ignoring Commission recommendations to DHS, the Commission noted a significant disconnect in the Department's planning response for nuclear terrorism." Dr. Frankel said that the DHS had allocated billions of dollars for sensors to find devices at ports of entry but "no discernible planning that considers whether the same nuclear device might not be launched from offshore to produce an EMP"[49].

There is reluctance to address the threat in other federal agencies too. The National Planning Scenarios for disaster response exercises do not include EMP. EMP is not considered a weapon of mass destruction.

---

[48] Dr. Frankel, Michael J., Statement *"Government Preparedness and Response to a Terrorist Attack Using Weapons of Mass Destruction"*, Subcommittee on Terrorism and Homeland Security, Senate Judiciary Committee, August 4, 2010

[49] Ibid

Does Congress understand the threat?

In a 1997 U.S. House, Subcommittee hearing, Dr. Gary L. Smith, detailed the EMP threat:

"..we have found the phenomenon is very real and well understood by the nuclear weapons effects community; … there would likely be pronounced effects on the civilian infrastructure from such a pulse; that the magnitude and extent of these effects is difficult even to estimate; and that it is probably not feasible to completely protect the entire infrastructure from the effects of such a pulse."[50]

As a result of scientific testimony about the threat, Congress authorized the EMP Commission in 2001 and again in 2006. The EMP Commission prepared classified reports and released two non-classified reports in 2004 and 2008. The 2004 Executive Report summarized the threat, "It is not surprising that a single EMP attack may well encompass and degrade at least 70% of the Nation's electrical service, all in one instant."[51]

The EMP Commission provided a plan that could protect the critical infrastructures from a nuclear or natural EMP catastrophe within 3-5 years and at a modest cost. [52] If Congress had responded, we would be at far less risk now.

After thirteen years of testimony, the U.S. House of Representatives passed the GRID Act in 2010 (HR5026).

---

[50] Smith, Dr. Gary L., Statement, *'Threat Posed by Electromagnetic Pulse (EMP) to U.S. Military Systems and Civil Infrastructure"*, Subcommittee on Military Research and Development", Committee on National Security, U.S. House July 16 1997, p 1

[51] Foster, Dr. John S, Earl Gjelde, Dr William R Graham et al, *Executive Summary,* Report of the Commission to Assess the Threat to the United States from Electromagnetic Pulse (EMP), Executive Report 2004, p18,.

[52] Graham, William, Statement, *"Securing the Modern Electric Grid from Physical and Cyber Attacks*, Subcommittee on Emerging Threats, Cybersecurity, and Science and Technology, Committee on Homeland Security, July 21, 2009 p11

It required the utilities to make necessary upgrades to protect the power grid from solar storms and electromagnetic disruptions, including intentional acts.

However, in the same month, August 2010, the U.S. Senate Energy Committee took out the reference to protection of the power grid from EMP events from their energy bill. The Senate Energy Committee hearings have not focused on grid protection. Instead they have held hearings on **Appliance Standards, Net Metering, Renewable Energy, Greenhouse Gas, and Climate Change**. These issues will be of little value when there is no power.

What is the Executive Branch's response to the EMP threat?

Dr. William R. Graham summarized in the 2008 EMP Commission Report "The Commission's view is that the Federal Government does not today have sufficient human and physical assets for reliably assessing and managing EMP threats."[53] The Commission Report on EMP was released on the same day as the 9/11 Commission Report. Attention continues to be focused on past threats instead of future threats.

A 2010 appointment of a missile defense critic and EMP Commission critic to the Associate Director for National Security and International Affairs at the White House Office of Science and Technology Policy may indicate the lack of regard for the EMP threat by the White House.

---

[53] Dr. Graham, William, Statement, *"Threat Posed by Electromagnetic Pulse Attack"*, House Armed Services Committee, July 10, 2008, p 6

Is the EMP threat a partisan issue?

The EMP Commission was bipartisan. The EMP Commission was established by a Republican Congress in 2001 and reauthorized by a Democratic Congress in 2006. The EMP Commissions determined that the man-made EMP threat is a danger to the U.S. The Commission's work was reviewed by members of the intelligence, all security agencies and the military community. [54] While those who promote EMP protection are bipartisan, those who oppose EMP protection are not.

What is the cost of hardening the civilian system from an EMP?

Ten years ago the cost of protecting the infrastructure was reported at $2 billion. The recent cost estimate to protect the grid was $5 to $10 billion.

The costs of hardening are inconsequential when compared to the cost of the potential damage; because a single EMP pulse could cause several trillion dollars[55] worth of damage.

Sadly, the current administration's economic stimulus plan provided **$4.5 billion for SmartGrid technology but not for EMP hardening.**

If an EMP attack or solar storm shuts down the power grid, very few Americans can earn a living. Private industry will virtually cease production until the power

---

[54] EMPACT America, "*Frequently Asked Questions*", http://wwww.empactamerica.org/faq.php printed 10/27/2010

[55] Dr Wood, Lowell, testimony, *Threat Posed by Electromagnetic Pulse to U.S. Military Systems and Civil Infrastructure,,*", U.S. House, Committee on National Security, July 16, 1997, p 46

can be restored. Financial transactions will not be possible except in a very limited paper based system.

Only a few jobs will continue unaffected, including power system workers, until the employees are unable to get to work because of lack of fuel for transportation.

When will an EMP event happen?

A major geomagnetic storm that could create EMP damage is expected within a few decades.

Potentially more imminent, rogue and hostile nations claim they have developed EMP weapons and they boast that they can wipe out the U.S. technologic advantage now. Perhaps they are already testing their missile launches near our coasts.

The U.S. has done little to protect the infrastructure from damage at this time. It would take three to five years to install the protective hardware, even if the industry or government decides to do so. Many scientists believe we are more vulnerable now than at any time in our past.

What is the expected mortality?

The U.S. has supported a current population of over 300 million because of our high standard of living, clean water, functioning sanitary systems, climate controlled shelter, and plentiful food. A large-scale attack will dissolve all of these qualities. The remaining resources could only support a fraction of our population.

If the U.S. remains a rural economy for an extended time, Dr. Graham testified, "We can go back to an era when people did live like that. That would be-10% would be 30 million people, and that is probably the range where we could survive as a basically rural economy."[56]

Based on this statement, 90% of our population could perish if the infrastructure is damaged for an extended time.

What can Americans do in preparation?

Surviving an EMP event will require the actions of individuals, because the Federal government is not protecting us. They have protected Air Force One, Navy Ships, and Nuclear Weapons against EMP, but our civilian power grid remains open and vulnerable.

Since the federal government is unwilling and unable to protect the power grid, it is up to individuals to:

1.   create a back up solar or wind power supply with battery bank for recharging batteries for essential communication and lighting equipment

2.   store sufficient food for a year

3.   create a plan for water supply procurement and purification

4.   create a plan for sewage waste collection and disposal

5.   create a safe fire proof and insect proof food storage and solar cooking system

6.   plan for heating a small space in a well ventilated area

---

[56] Dr. Graham, William, *"Threat Posed by Electromagnetic Pulse Attack*, U.S. House Armed Services Committee, July 10, 2008 p 9

7. stock survival supplies for a wide range of daily living needs, including self defense

8. obtain an amateur radio license and battery powered equipment

9. seek training in first aid, disease management, plant identification, alternative medicine, simple electronics, sanitation, fire safety and self defense weapons

10. store all required electrical equipment in improvised faraday cages

11. accumulate gold, junk silver or small survival items for bartering during the crisis

12. accumulate extra provisions for charitable giving

What can you do to encourage national attention to an EMP threat?

Contact your Senators and Representatives and let them know of your concern about the electrical power grid. Visit the website of EMPact America for scientific updates on the threat. According to the website, they are a non profit organization for citizens concerned about protection from a nuclear or natural EMP catastrophe. The website states their mission is to: re-establish the EMP Commission, implement the EMP Commission recommendations to protect the civilian infrastructures, educate the American people on the threat and actions necessary, and initiate pilot programs to increase EMP preparedness.

They were not consulted for this book, but we support and encourage their efforts.

Chapter Two
The Power Grid

"Should the electrical power system be lost for any substantial period of time, the Commission believes that the consequences are likely to be catastrophic to civilian society. Machines will stop; transportation and communication will be severely restricted; heating, cooling and lighting will cease; food and water supplies will be interrupted; and many people may die."[57]

Perhaps because of the history of only short term power grid failures following storms, power outages are considered a problem of inconvenience, instead of a crisis. The widespread EMP electrical outages could be disastrous. Millions of Americans may wait for hours, days, months or years for power restoration. The little food, fuel and water they stored will be depleted and they will be a refugee like millions of others before the power is restored. When the power is eventually restored, America may not be the same. Even geographic areas that escape the EMP will be affected by desperate refugees.

Optimism is part of the American spirit. We assume that repairs will be completed and the power restored. We have never had to reverse our forward progress in technology. However, the early technological advances of

---

[57] Dr. Foster, John S. Jr,, Mr. Earl Gjelde, et al, "*Critical National Infrastructures*", Report of the Commission to Assess the Threat to the United States from Electromagnetic Pulse Attack, April 2008, p 18

decades past are long forgotten and the parts have been discarded. The newer and advanced equipment and parts are often not even manufactured in the U.S. How will the scientists, electric technicians and the parts suppliers plan a repair strategy with no telecommunications and no transportation?

The 2008 "Critical National Infrastructures", Report of the EMP Commission thoroughly analyzed the vulnerabilities to a widespread event. They found the system was unprotected and repairs would be difficult to complete.

"Some critical electrical power infrastructure components are no longer manufactured in the United States and their acquisition ordinarily requires up to a year of lead time in routine circumstances. Damage to or loss of these components could leave significant parts of the electrical infrastructure out of service for periods measured in months to a year or more." [58]

What is the power grid?

The U.S. continental electrical grid is divided into two large geographic zones of regional service. A cascading power failure could cease service to at least half the nation. Each zone has a patchwork of public, private and cooperative utility companies.

The following is a graphic illustrating the power grid composition.

---

[58] Dr. Foster, John S., et al "Critical National Infrastructures", Report of the Commission to Assess the Threat, April 2008 preface, vi

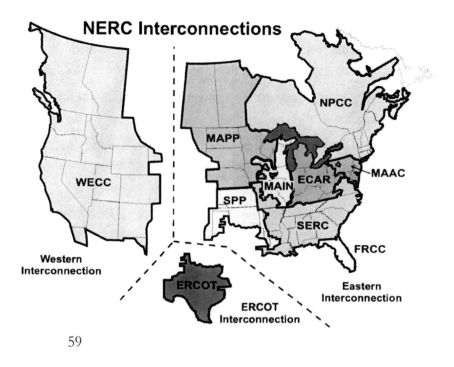

NERC Interconnections

59

The power industry is the foundation of our American civilization. Our lifestyle can quickly degrade to a third world status without power. Our survival is even more tenuous than in primitive cultures, because we no longer have skills in survival and we rely too much on electronics.

Why is a long term power grid failure probable?

---

[59] Dr. Foster, John S., *"Critical National Infrastructures"* Report of the Commission to Assess the Threat, April 2008, Figure 2-2 NERC Interconnections, p 25

A long term power grid failure is probable because the system is:

1. susceptible because of the sophistication and dependence on electronic parts

2. currently operating beyond generation capacity margins

3. expanded with newer plants built farther from the customers, creating miles of exposed transmission lines

4. reliant on newer supplemental sources like wind and solar that create unpredictable streams of energy

5. neglected in large parts of the transmission system that are not profit generating

6. remotely managed and controlled by vulnerable electronic systems

7. reliant on transformers made overseas that have a one to three year backlog to produce even without a power grid disaster

8. newer transformers are more vulnerable because they rely on single phase instead of triple phase for purposes of shipping. Older transformers built in the U.S. were larger.

9. there are no energy storage capabilities.

Why is our power grid vulnerable?

The power grid owners believe they have secondary systems to protect the power grid, but they have not been evaluated for EMP damage. They have been evaluated for a wide range of other, lesser threats. No one will know if the secondary systems are sufficient until they are tested by an EMP attack.

The power industry has protections against lightning strikes and other lesser hazards but they probably will not prevent the damage of an EMP. Neither natural phenomena nor any other nuclear weapon effects are so widespread.[60]

The damage to electronics will depend on protective shielding. Currently our civilian power grid is not protected from an EMP.

Why doesn't the industry research the vulnerabilities and protections against EMP?

The EMP risk is classified in the industry as "low-probability, high consequence."

85% of the civilian power industry is privately controlled and the standards are set by the industry. The electric industry invests little in research and development compared to other industries and has been reluctant to make the investment for hardening of their system.

They do not even invest in surplus inventory large transformers or support the manufacturing of the transformers in the U.S., to insure availability. The Research and Development (R&D) investment of the energy industry in the U.S. is reported to be .3%. Among

[60] Dr. Smith, Gary L., Statement, "Threat Posed by Electromagnetic Pulse to U.S. Military Systems and Civil Infrastructure, Military Research and Development Subcommittee, July 16, 1997 p 3

all industries, research and development expenses average 3% of GDP. That is ten times more than the energy industry. This also compares to 15% R&D investment in the medical and biotechnology field, or 40 times more than the energy industry. [61]

"Today the existing electrical system at peak demand periods increasingly operates at or near reliability limits of its physical capacity."[62]

U.S. Representative, Yvette D. Clarke, chair of a U.S. House Subcommittee, in her opening statement said "It is amazing that many within the industry would gamble with our national and economic security than implement precautionary security measures. ...I am at a loss to explain why the industry isn't appropriately securing its assets."[63]

According to one witness statement, the North American Electric Reliability Corporation, (NERC) standards are largely created and approved by industry and are somewhat self policing.[64]

[61] Dr. Kammen, Daniel M., *"Investing in the Future: R and D Needs to Meet America's Energy and Climate Challenges"*, Select Committee on Energy Independence and Global Warming, U.S. House, September 10, 2008 , http://docs.google.com globalwarming.house.gov/tools

[62] Dr. Foster, John S., *"Critical National Infrastructures"*, Report of the Commission to Assess the Threat, April 2008, page 17,18

[63] Rep. Clarke, Yvette D. Opening Statement, *"Securing the Modern Electric Grid from Physical and Cyber Attacks"*, Subcommittee on Emerging Threats, Cybersecurity and Science and Technology, Committee on Homeland Security, July 21, 2009.

[64] Ahern, Brian, Statement for the Record, *"Securing the Modern Electric Grid from Physical and Cyber Attacks"*, Subcommittee on Emerging Threats, Cybersecurity and Science and Technology, Committee on Homeland Security, July 21, 2009 statement, p 4

Representative Yvette Clarke, said that "many in the electric industry are apparently trying to avoid compliance with their own inadequate standards".[65]

Do they plan on protecting the power grid?

The electric industry regulating group, NERC, warns that the protection of the grid will be costly and require a lot of time. They are currently conducting workshops to discuss the issue.

Representatives from industry testified that there should be cost recovery for utilities to reimburse expenses through rate payers. Mr. Joseph H. McClelland, Director of Reliability, Federal Energy Regulatory Commission, testified to a Subcommittee based on his experience in the electric utility industry and government that "but the chance that industry would move forward, if it considers it to be a low probability of event, with everything else that is happening, is really not realistic."[66]

At a hearing of the U.S. House Subcommittee on Emerging Threats, Cyber Security, Brian M. Ahern, reported, "There is a risk that industries that do not have compliance mandates may be willing to play percentages that a critical infrastructure incident will not happen at their company, rather than spend thousands or millions of dollars to mitigate any known risks and vulnerabilities."[67]

---

[65] Rep. Clarke, Yvette D, Opening Statement, ,"*Securing the Modern Electric Grid from Physical and Cyber Attacks*", Subcommittee on Emerging Threats, Cybersecurity, and Science and Technology, Committee on Homeland Security, July 21 2009

[66] McClelland, Joseph H., Testimony, "*Securing the Modern Electric Grid from Physical and Cyber Attacks*", Subcommittee on Emerging Threats, Cybersecurity and Science and Technology, Committee on Homeland Security, July 21, 2009 p75

[67] Ahern, Brian, Statement for the Record, "*Securing the Modern Electric Grid from Physical and Cyber Attacks*", Subcommittee on Emerging Threats, Cybersecurity and Science and Technology, Committee on Homeland Security, July 21, 2009 statement, p 1

The power industry has been reluctant to address the EMP threat. Public statements suggest a perceived low risk within the industry and a reluctance to invest in their own infrastructure.

> "... A single EMP attack may seriously degrade or shut down a large part of the electric power grid in the geographic area of EMP exposure effectively instantaneously. There is also a possibility of functional collapse of grids beyond the exposed area, as electrical effects propagate from one region to another."[68]

Why isn't EMP hardening demanded?

The industry, with the support of the federal government, is prioritizing expenses and unfortunately, EMP protection is not a high priority for the industry or government.

On October 27, 2009, the acting Assistant Secretary for Electricity Delivery and Energy Reliability at the U.S. Department of Energy, testified before a U.S. House Committee, "improving the resiliency of the Nation's electric power grid for the purpose of national security comes at a cost... As Congress considers legislation, we recognize there are limited resources. Therefore, we must prioritize based on risk, impact to the electric system and cost constraints."[69]

---

[68] Dr. Foster, John S. *"Critical National Infrastructures"*, Report of the Commission to Assess the Threat to the United States from Electromagnetic Pulse, July 10,2008 preface p vi

[69] Hoffman, Patricia, Statement, to the Energy and Commerce Committee, Energy and Environment Subcommittee, U.S. House of Representatives, October 27, 2009 p 1

She added "Over the last 6 months the Department has been highly focused on implementing several initiatives set forth in the Recovery Act, including $4.5 Billion for smart grid activities designed to jumpstart the modernization of the electric power grid, reduce electricity use, reduce greenhouse gas emissions, and spur innovation and economic recovery."[70]

Unfortunately, the SmartGrid project does not address EMP protection. The Stimulus Act dedicated $4,500,000,000 for SmartGrid technologies, a clean energy initiative, not an EMP hardening effort. Further, the SmartGrid adds even more digital technology that is potentially vulnerability to attack.

Mr. Sean P. McGurk, Director, Control Systems Security Program, Office of Cybersecurity and Communications, Department of Homeland Security, testified at a U.S. House Subcommittee hearing in 2009, "...but the reality is that the more effective we are in producing a Smart Grid, the less secure we are from an EMP attack. Because that just increases our vulnerability."[71]

While war strategists in other nations are boasting about a new generation of super-EMP's, we haven't even started protecting our infrastructure. Our investments increase the system vulnerabilities.

Significant elements of the system, including many generating plants are aging, (a considerable number are more than 50 years old) and becoming less reliable or are

---

[70] Ibid, p 4

[71] McGurk, Sean P., Testimony, "*Securing the Modern Electric Grid from Physical and Cyber Attacks*", Subcommittee on Emerging Threats Cybersecutity and Sciences and Technology, Committee on Homeland Security, July 21, 2009 p 79

under pressure to be retired for environmental considerations, further exacerbating the situation."[72]

How difficult is it to restart the power grid?

Restarting the grid will be a complicated and long term process. To restart, they will need power. The power to restart may not be available for a long distance. The power could come from "blackstart" units. The problem is there are few blackstart units available.

The EMP Commission found that the electric industry has no plans for black-starting the national power grid in the event of a continent-wide collapse.[73]

Before restarting, the damaged parts must be identified, ordered, manufactured and shipped from overseas and replaced. This must be accomplished by crews with no fuel for transportation and no phone service to communicate. The backup generators will be exhausted before the restart can occur.

In addition, the measuring equipment, calibration and controls necessary to reset the grid will also be affected by an EMP. Lack of calibration can make restarting the grid dangerous.

"Over the last decade or two, relatively few new large-capacity electric transmission capabilities have been

[72]Dr. Foster, John S., "*Critical National Infrastructures*", Report of the Commission to Assess the Threat, April 2008 pp. 17,18

[73] Dr. Pry, Peter Vincent, "*Terrorism and the EMP Threat to Homeland Security*", U.S. Senate, Committee on the Judiciary, Subcommittee on Terrorism, Technology and Homeland Security, p 15

constructed and most of the additions to generation transmission capacity that have been made have been located considerable distances from load for environmental, political and economic reasons, adding stress and further limiting the system's ability to withstand disruption.[74]

---

[74] Ibid

Chapter Three
Power and Our Way of Life

How dependent are we on the power grid?

A widespread power outage will result in a catastrophe because our entire way of life is dependent on power. We do not have the knowledge or experience to survive without power. The widespread power outage will affect:

1. fuel, because gas station refueling depends on electrical pumps.

2. automobiles, because some vehicles will not restart. Electronics have been built into cars for decades.

2. water and sewage systems, because the treatment plants are dependent on electrical pumps.

3. safe meat or dairy foods, spoiled within hours of loss of refrigeration.

4. communication by telephone, cell service or 911 emergency services, if large antenna are rendered inoperable and after backup generators run out of 72 hours of stored generator power.

5. traffic control, because of no traffic light power and many stalled vehicles out of fuel on the roads.

6. personal safety, when millions of hungry and stressed refugees seek food, water and shelter from others. Millions of urban dwellers will be hiking into the country to escape the uninhabitable conditions within the cities.

7. health concerns, will revert to communicable diseases of the last century. Dysentery, tetanus, typhus and cholera will cause acute morbidity and mortality.

8. fires, widespread because of gas line leaks, open fires for heating and cooking, arson, and lack of water or equipment to fight these fires.

> "Because of the ubiquitous dependence of U.S. society on the electrical power system, its vulnerability to an EMP attack, coupled with the EMP's particular damage mechanisms creates the possibility of long term catastrophic consequences." [75]

Part Two in this book will describe the preparations that we made ourselves, in the event of an EMP attack. We are not certain it will occur, but it is reasonable for all Americans to prepare. It is easier and cheaper to acquire the survival training, equipment and provisions now, rather than later. Once prepared, families can relax, appreciate and enjoy the technology while it is still available.

---

[75] Dr. Foster, John S. Jr., Mr. Earl Gjelde, Dr. William R Graham,, Dr. Robert J Hermann et al, "*Critical National Infrastructures*", Report of the Commission to Assess the Threat to the United States from Electromagnetic Pulse (EMP)Attack, April 2008, preface, p. vi.

PART TWO

EMP SURVIVAL

It is our sincere hope that after the preparation, you will never need to use these provisions because the EMP event never occurs. No one can predict how large an event it may be. We based our survival needs on one year without power. Some scientists say it could be longer.

We cover the basic preparations in this book for essential needs. Your family needs, community demographic, your geography and climate may require special preparation. This book is an overview of the basics. The details are limited so it is important to find additional texts on each survival activity.

You will want to have texts in your survival library about plant identification, food preservation, first aid, disease control, outdoor survival, battery bank installation, wiring, alternative energy, medicine, alternative medicine, and self defense weaponry. You will want to acquire the books and visit the websites as soon as possible on the Recommended Reading list in the Appendix.

To assist in your planning and purchasing we included a Supplies List in the Appendix. You should adjust and add to this list based on your needs. You will want to have a large quantity of most items on the list. We also included an appendix with a checklist of tasks to prepare for survival. You will want to practice using the methods described.

This book is based on our reading of survival preparation texts and congressional testimony of EMP-related hearings, combined with our experience and training. We have had careers in electrical engineering, holistic nutrition and public health sanitation. We have no specific training in survival, but we have spent the last six months in preparation.

Details of our plans for surviving in our home one year without power are provided as an example. We have created two survival locations, equally equipped, one in our suburban Chicago home and one in our weekend retreat home. We have made the purchases for the equipment we describe and we detail our sources and the estimated costs. We have calculated the quantity of batteries, food and water that will be needed.

The intent is to describe our preparation, research and purchasing experience so that readers can benefit from our effort. We hope that readers will further research and enhance these plans and options for their situation. If readers discover more valuable survival information we hope they will be motivated to provide that information to the public.

The EMP survivalist must have some expertise in areas of communication, medicine, first aid, wild foods, solar energy, and electronics. **Training, or at minimum, a good library of information should be acquired before the event.** The following is the expertise that will be needed:

1. Food- Food Supplies should be procured to feed your family for a year. Food should be packaged for long term storage and selected based on nutrition preservation. Raw wheat is one of the best options for preserving nutrition and economy. Primitive survival food preparation options and equipment will be briefly described.

2. Wild foods- when the emergency foods stored for the disaster are depleted, stolen, or confiscated you need to know where and how to procure natural foods. Food sources in trees, weeds and berries are abundant. A text on identifying and preparing wild food is critical. Wild plants can also pose a health risk due to allergy or natural poisons. Some plants contain natural cyanide or arsenic. Make certain that you have a plant identification guide for your area. The U.S. Department of Army <u>Illustrated Guide to Edible Wild Plants</u> is an excellent reference.

3. Water- Equipment for collecting and purifying water should be purchased. A five gallon plastic pail with a lid or five gallon plastic tank with a cap, labeled for drinking only will be useful for daily collection. Purification will involve boiling or chlorinating.

4. Communication- an amateur radio license and battery operated equipment to provide emergency outreach and world wide news will be very useful. Family and friends may be able to communicate knowing frequencies, times, and call signs in advance. Battery-operated shortwave radio equipment for world news and

local CB radios for local patrols are in the equipment list.

5. Faraday Cages- Electronics technical knowledge will be useful for preparing improvised "faraday cages" to protect electronics from the EMP. If there is an EMP attack or solar storm, only electronics stored in a "faraday cage" will continue to work. An improvised faraday cage is essentially a plastic lined metal box into which you place the electronic equipment. These protective shielding devices can be purchased or constructed and will be discussed later in the book.

6. Energy-Solar energy panels or wind turbines will be necessary to recharge batteries and for essential lighting and cooking power. Solar food cookers are very effective. This book will provide the essentials of solar power and solar cooking. In some settings, wind power may be a reasonable alternative.

7. Heat- Wood burning stoves or propane heaters can be the source of heat. A small room can be heated in the basement with sufficient ventilation to sustain the family for a winter.

8. Security- Self defense weapons and training is essential for survival.

9. Medicine- essential medicine should be stored in adequate supplies for emergencies. When the medicine is depleted and prescriptions are not available, alternative options for treatment should be known. A U.S. Army <u>Medical Handbook</u> will be a necessary survival

reference. Some natural remedies are very effective. We identify some remedies recommended by several independent sources.

10. First Aid- first aid training from the Red Cross and a family emergency guide will be necessary for reference. Keep a large supply of first aid bandages, disinfectants and ointments for the expected injuries from the intensive hard labor required to survive. There will be increased risk of fire, cuts, heat and cold exposure and stings.

11. Sanitation-Equipment for collecting and disposing of waste should be prepared. A five gallon plastic pail and plastic disposable liners will be used for indoor toilet waste. A shovel will be needed for disposal of the bags on a daily basis. When weather permits, outdoor latrine construction is preferred.

12. Religion- Prayer and biblical principles will allow survivors to persevere in survival circumstances and deep personal loss.

U.S. Representative Roscoe Bartlett said "I am very concerned that if we as individuals and families do not know what to do and are not prepared, that every one of us then becomes a ward of the state". He then asked, "And are we not enormously stronger if we are individually and family wise self sufficient during an emergency like that?"[76]

---

[76] Bartlett, Roscoe, *"Threat Posed by Electromagnetic Pulse Attack"*, U.S. House Armed Services Committee, July 10, 2008, p 28

Chapter Four
What You Need to Do

How will you know if it is an EMP outage or a routine storm related short term power outage?

If your radio does not work, check for broadcast radio stations on your crank powered radio that was stored in a faraday cage for protection. Some of the clues will be: if there is no radio transmission, if many cars are stranded on the road and will not restart, or if even some of your battery operated appliances will not work. If you observe these occurrences, then it may be an EMP catastrophe.

How will you know how extensive the outage is?

Battery operated and faraday protected amateur radios, short wave radios and police scanners may first provide evidence of how extensive the power outage is. The wider the outage, the longer the power may remain out.

What will you do first?

If you determine it may be an EMP, the first priority will be to assemble your family and any others you want to protect and activate your pre-arranged plan for survival and evacuation. You should have already established a list of communication options with those family members. You should also have established alternative meeting locations and time schedules, in case communication is not possible.

Because an EMP may affect communication and transportation, these plans must be prepared in advance with many contingencies, redundancies and alternatives.

What decisions will you need to make about evacuation?

Your pre-arranged evacuation plans must include:

1. whether to escape an urban home for a pre-stocked country retreat.

2. sufficient motor fuel procured for the entire trip to the retreat location.

3. arrangements for meeting other family members in multiple scenarios.

4. communication plans and alternatives with family and friends..

5. emergency police scanners with pre-programmed county channels to determine safe evacuation routes.

6. long term survival provisions already in place with redundancies.

7. a pre-packed emergency escape backpack with maps, food, water, blankets, tools

Can you evacuate safely immediately?

Those who are unprepared when the power grid fails may head to the local markets for food and supplies, if their car starts. Unfortunately, they will not be successful, because the stores won't have power or inventory. They will waste their remaining fuel in the effort.

Those who have previously stockpiled supplies can leave an urban area. There will be a short window of opportunity for departure if you have a remote country location supplied and ready for survival. Those who have prepared for the power loss should be safely on the road before the unprepared leave their homes with insufficient food, water or fuel. We plan to pack our bikes in the car so that if the roads are blocked we can pedal the rest of the way.

If you do not already have a stocked destination, it may be better to stay home unless you know the catastrophe is limited to your community. Urban residents should probably plan to leave immediately.

The roads may be blocked with stalled cars. The EMP commission reports that 90% of the cars will restart. Other foreign source research reports are not as promising.

What issues will interfere with evacuation?

Within a few days or hours it may be too late to make a fast and efficient exit from the city. Fuel will not be available because gas pumps require electricity. You may use your hand siphon device to transfer gas from one of your vehicles to another.

The roads may be jammed with stalled cars with insufficient fuel. The bridges may be particularly difficult to pass, later in the evacuation, if local residents want to prevent evacuees from entering their area by the bridge.

Communication with family members will be difficult and may delay your evacuation. Alternative meeting time and place arrangements should be made in advance to enable early evacuation.

A portable battery powered police scanner with county emergency channels pre-programmed will assist in the evacuation. These emergency channels for each county can be found on the internet.

Before you leave your home, you will want to monitor road conditions on your police scanner and amateur radio. If your portable police scanner reveals congestion and chaos on the highways you may consider the secondary roads. You should have local county maps for each county between you and your stocked retreat.

How many evacuees will there be?

We predict there will be a massive evacuation of urban residents to the rural areas. As an example, the 9,000,000 population of the Chicago metropolitan area would average 155 urban evacuees on every square mile of Illinois. Currently, there are only 67 people residing on every square mile of Illinois outside of the metro area. **That means, on average, there will be three times as many evacuees as residents in the rural parts of the**

State. The evacuees would be desperately seeking water, food and shelter.

Why will urban dwellers evacuate, even without preparation?

High rise apartment buildings will have no water pumps from the beginning of the crisis. Toilets won't flush, and sewer lines are empty allowing rats to enter through pipes. The stagnant, untreated sewage will enter surface water streams during the next rain. The surface waters, i.e. rivers and lakeshores, in the city will be quickly contaminated by human waste.

After two hours without refrigeration, potentially hazardous foods (meats, dairy, poultry, and fish) will begin to grow toxic organisms. Flies, whose lifecycle have always depended on our putrefied waste, will proliferate. The exposed spoiled food and human waste will increase the risk of flies transmitting diseases.

Emergency call centers will be unable to function initially due to huge demand and later due to back up power outage. Desperate and possibly armed mobs will seek food and fuel from anyone who still has a supply. The loss of lighting and security devices will increase the security risk.

The urban refugees will be on their own to find food, water, shelter and security, competing with millions of others. Is it any question they will leave for the open country to escape?

What is a good retreat location?

A survival retreat home 200 miles from a large city and within a tank of gas will be ideal. This will be a one way trip. **Your retreat must be within the range of your gas tank.** There will be no fuel during your trip. If you have considered purchasing a retreat home, now would be a good time in preparation of an EMP event. The retreat home should be completely stocked in advance.

If you have two cars, keep them both half filled with fuel. Be aware that some cars are equipped with anti siphon devices. You can carry a hand siphon device on your trip to extract gas from disabled vehicles while on the road.

It is critical to communicate with your family before you leave, if you do not already have a plan. You may not be able to communicate again unless you have neighbors with amateur radio equipment at both locations and you know the time and frequency of transmission.

One basic contingency is to leave a written note at a pre-arranged location with coded evacuation plans. Community postings could be the primary method of long distance communication for individuals through amateur radio operators.

What is the risk of staying in the suburban home?

If we miss the evacuation opportunity we will stay in our equally equipped suburban home. The risk of staying in the suburban home is the intrusion of urban refugees seeking food and shelter.

The advantage of the suburban community is the opportunity to create survival teams leading the community in group survival. Skills and expertise among residents in the community can be utilized as team leaders for self defense, carpentry, sanitation, communication, first aid and food foraging and preparation.

The millions of evacuees from the urban areas will drive until they reach the stalled traffic and then they will be on foot. They can walk at least 10 miles a day. Any homes within sight of the highway could be searched and scavenged. Some houses may be used as bonfires for heat. Unprepared evacuees will be desperate for food, water and shelter. Even the retreat location 200 miles away can expect refugees within 20 days.

The refugees may discover your shelter and provisions. You may consider hiding your survival supplies behind fireproof false walls, in a buried compartment or in fireproof containers, camouflaged as paperwork.

Communication equipment that allows you to listen to other broadcasts will assist in determining the level of crime and the level of self-defense required. You must already be supplied with the level of defense that you need. Self defense weapons will be discussed later.

What is the risk of evacuating to the retreat?

During our evacuation, if no road is passable, we may hike toward our stocked retreat. Backpacks with food, water, blanket, waterproof sheet, candles, local county maps, compass, mirror, whistle, antiseptic, bandages, metal cup for boiling water, extra clothes, and matches have already been prepared and stored in the car. Also, we have police scanners and CB's in the car, stored in faraday cages.

If you must abandon the vehicle, because it is stolen or confiscated and you are forced to hike, use the compass or known roads. If you become lost, you will want to follow a straight line toward your destination. A trick to walk a straight line on a cloudy day is to spot three points ahead in the distance and re-spot three more before you reach the first one

Remember that you can walk three miles an hour and in some circumstances that is your fastest way out of an urban area. A bicycle will allow ten to twenty miles an hour.

Chapter Five
Food Supplies

Based on the recent history of power outages during major storms, the grocery stores will be emptied within hours. The average home supply of food will be emptied within days to two weeks.

> "Today, cities typically have a food supply of only several days available on grocery shelves for their customers."[77]

Initially, the lack of refrigeration will result in dairy, poultry, fish and meats (potentially hazardous foods) that must be quickly consumed before bacteria make it unsafe to eat. Food in the freezers will remain frozen for one day, and a chest freezer will remain frozen for two days. You can prolong this by adding snow or ice to the freezer, if your climate provides it.

The potentially hazardous foods must be eaten within two hours of reaching 41F degrees and above. This is known as the "time and temperature danger zone". Beyond the time and temperature danger zone, you could ingest bacteria and toxins that could cause diarrhea and vomiting for days and eventual death, due to dehydration and electrolyte imbalance. The medical supplies will include oral rehydration salts for this reason.

---

[77] Dr. Foster, John S., *"Critical National Infrastructures"*, Report of the Commission to Assess the Threat, April 2008 p 112

For added safety, even if the foods are within the time and temperature safety zone, cook the thawed meat and dairy foods thoroughly before eating. Some bacteria produce a toxin that can survive boiling, so this is not necessarily a safe method.

Canned or dried packaged meats or dairy originally sold un-refrigerated on the store shelves is safe to eat. Butter, eggs in unbroken shells, and packaged dried meat sold un-refrigerated may be safe to eat also.

Hard salami-type cured meats and hard cheeses may be safe to eat beyond the time and temperature danger zone.

Food that has a bad odor is unsafe to eat. Food that does not have a bad odor may still be unsafe. Bacteria that cause illness will not necessarily cause the food to smell or taste spoiled. Two to five days after the power outage thousands could be sickened with dehydration and electrolyte imbalance from severe diarrhea and vomiting by eating food that was un-refrigerated for too long.

When the refrigerated or frozen supply is depleted or outside the time and temperature danger zone, it is time to advance to your emergency provisions.

"If urban food supply flow is substantially interrupted for an extended period of time, hunger and mass evacuation, even starvation and anarchy could result."[78]

"Compared to blackouts, an EMP attack could inflict damage over a wider geographic area and damage a much

---

[78] Dr. Foster, John S. Jr, et al, *"Critical National Infrastructures"*, April 2008 p112

wider array of equipment; consequently, recovery of the food infrastructure from EMP is likely to be much more complicated and more protracted."[79]

"Infrastructure failure at the level of food distribution because of disruption of the transportation system, as is likely during an EMP attack, could bring on food shortages affecting the general population in as little as 24 hours."[80]

During this crisis we will be eating for nutritional needs, not culinary quality.

Our basic emergency food supply comes in large, commercial size (#10 size) cans of wheat, oats, and pinto beans from the Church of Jesus Christ of Latter Day Saints (LDS). There are other good sources of survival foods available also.

Two pounds of food per person per day is sufficient for a survival supply. A year's supply of food for one person costs approximately $800. The cans prevent oxidation to a greater degree than other storage packaging. The cans should be stored below 70 degrees and can last up to 30 years.

Since 1936, the LDS church leaders pronounced that their membership should maintain a year's supply of food in the home in case of a disaster.

They do not charge for shipping and the price of the food is reasonable. You can visit www.ldscatalog.com to order the food or www.providentliving.org. for more

---

[79] Dr. Foster, John S., *"Critical National Infrastructures"*, Report of the Commission to Assess the Threat, April 2008 p 136

[80] Dr. Foster, John S., *"Critical National Infrastructures"*, Report of the Commission to Assess the Threat, April 2008 p 136

information about food storage. Apparently there is no issue with non members purchasing the products.

Why wheat?

Wheat retains the most nutrition after long storage. Wheat is less expensive in a raw state than other grains per pound. One cup of grain will serve two. The wheat is shipped in 33 pound boxes containing six 5.5 pound cans.

Wheat can be ground into flour and baked or fried or boiled and simmered. You can do the same with oats, beans, rice and corn. The raw grain can be boiled for 20 minutes then soaked overnight for soft, thick wheat berries that can be eaten as cereal. It can be fried with oil as a side dish. We cooked a cup of raw wheat in water in our homemade solar cooker in a small canning jar for three hours to produce soft cereal. We fried the raw wheat grains in oil on the stove for a great tasting snack.

Dried wheat, oats and beans will provide the bulk of our survival diet because they contain plenty of calories. Sufficient caloric intake will be critical to allow the important work tasks of security, warmth and water carrying.

The raw wheat grains can be hand milled twice, mixed with equal parts water and fried in oil for at least three minutes. The resulting flat-cake resembles a cookie. If a little sugar is added it could be used for survival celebrations.

The purchase of a hand grinder will allow you to make bread recipes. This cast iron Corn, Grain, Cereal Mill cost about $22.

If you don't have a hand grinder, use a stone in a bowl to crush and mix the seeds to a powder. You may also try a hammer to crush the seeds.

Beans

Raw beans should soak overnight in four parts water to one part beans. They should be boiled and then simmered for three hours. Adding vinegar will help with digestion. Adding fennel or cumin spices reportedly will reduce intestinal gas.

We have experimented with soaking dried beans in water, in case there is no source of heat to cook. After two days they are soft enough to eat. However, in four days, they smelled and were discarded. Experimenting in advance is important to avoid losing food when it is scarce.

Rice or beans can also be ground into flour, mixed with water, rolled flat and cut into noodles. In our tests, we needed to mill the flour more than three times. The flour after two hand milling cycles was too coarse to absorb the water.

Long term storage food from LDS

Sprouted Seeds

Sprouted seeds of grains, beans, peas and lentils can provide enzyme nutrition during the winter months when there are few green edible plants.

Sprouting seeds in a wet paper towel may be as successful as our trial following a standard process. We placed seeds in a glass jar and added three times more water as seeds. We let the seeds soak for 12 hours in a covered jar. After soaking and draining, we kept the sprouts in jars in a slanted position in a warm 65 degree, basement. They were supposed to sprout in three to five days. They didn't. This is another project to experiment before the emergency need. Find a good book on seed sprouting and experiment.

Is this all the food I need to survive?

To supplement this basic supply of nutrients, we have accumulated canned salmon, mackerel, sardines and tuna. Enhancing the survival diet with Omega 3 oils, available in fish is important for health. We have found a variety of discount stores have been good sources of canned fish. Essential fats like olive oil and less expensive canola oil were purchased in gallon quantities for food preparation. **A balance of Omega 3 and Omega 6 rich oils is essential for health.**

To insure adequate essential fat intake we also purchased gallon cans of olive oil.

In addition to the grains, beans, oil, and canned fish, we have stocked cases of canned vegetables and soups when they were priced well. In addition to these basic and nutritious foods we have an ample supply of iodized salt, baking powder, baking soda and some sugar in order to create primitive breads.

Pasta, cereal and oatmeal were purchased and stored in new metal garbage cans with tight fitting lids to prevent oxidation and prevent rodent infestation.

What about salt requirements?

Ordinarily, we get plenty of salt from our food. Our survival food supply will provide far less salt. Salt is one of the body's electrolytes that regulate our heart rate and other critical functions. Iodized salt is our primary source of iodine, an essential nutrient. We should maintain a supply of iodized salt to add to our survival food dishes.

If we perspire during strenuous labor, especially in hot weather, we will lose salt. Salt loss may cause heat cramps. A remedy for salt loss is to drink a glass of lightly salted water (.01%).

In order to make a .01% salt water solution follow two steps; First, mix ½ teaspoon of salt in 8 ounces of water, then mix only ½ teaspoon of this salted water solution in another 8 ounces of plain water. (.01% is 144 grains of salt, a fraction of a teaspoon)

Should you collect seeds for planting?

Vegetable gardens will provide the best nutrition. If you have bad luck with gardening, we suggest collard greens and yellow squash. In spite of weeds and droughts and bad soil, they have always done well in our garden.

Seeds may last three to five years. Seeds of squash, collard greens, turnips and spinach could be saved for five years.

You can test the germination rate by starting a few seeds in a wet paper towel and watching for growth.

If you are new to gardening, these are a few suggestions; read and follow the seed packet instructions, do not shock the seeds with cold water when you plant them, plant seeds in wet soil that is warmed by the sun, do not plant them too deeply and fertilize the garden soil with wood ashes for mineral nutrition.

Seeds are available as F1, hybrids and heirloom. F1 hybrids are the engineered seeds the farmer's plant, they produce large, uniform crops the first generation and are inferior in subsequent generations.

Heirloom seeds produce hardier, smaller, not as uniform plants, intended to allow you to use seeds from your plant to grow the same quality produce the following years. Heirloom seeds are from varieties grown since 1950.

You can use the seeds from your own vegetable plantings. Harvested seeds should be allowed to mature in the plant, then removed and dried and stored in an air tight glass jar.

Based on our reading, all vegetable seeds can be harvested and if stored properly will produce vegetables. Any seed may reproduce. If the seed is not labeled as F1 or Hybrid, the seed will produce hardier subsequent generations of vegetables.

Potatoes and the bulbs of green onions should be stored in a dark cool place and kept from freezing to re-plant in the spring.

How do you store the fresh foods?

To preserve foods you can: keep them cold, smoke and cure, salt, dehydrate, jelly, pickle or can. The following is a brief summary of the treatments we have read. You need to study detailed instructions and experiment before attempting to preserve survival food.

Potentially hazardous foods, meat, poultry, fish and dairy, especially, require careful preparation to avoid food borne illnesses. Salt, sugar, vinegar, dehydration, heat and smoke all have some bacteria inhibiting qualities in varying degrees. Historical recipes of food preservation often use a combination of treatments. The jars used for food storage should be sanitized with the bleach solution described later or rinsed with boiling water before adding the food.

There are several methods described for salting and smoking. Most require several days of treatment. It is important to study these methods in preparation. In most descriptions of smoking meats a combination of salting and smoking is utilized. According to preparations we have read, lean meats should be sliced thin and stored over alternating layers of salt for days, then the thin slices are placed over a wood fire to smoke. A metal or wooden rack could be improvised over a campfire. The temperature should maintain 125 to 150 degrees. A "dome" could be placed over the food to retain the heat and smoke. The smoke is effective in destroying bacteria on the exterior of the meat but does not penetrate to the inside of the meat.

Primitive Indians, pirates and sailors made a dried meat snack called pemmican. Based on the historical descriptions, they pounded the lean meat thin, dried it in the sun or over a campfire for two days, added melted fat and mixed in wild berries. The entire mixture was compressed and closed in an air tight container. According to our reading, to avoid rancidity in stored meats, remove the fat before preparation and add the fat back only after rendering (chopping, melting by simmering and straining).

Vegetables can be pickled with salt and vinegar. They should be peeled, thoroughly soaked with salted water for two days. The vegetables are then covered with salted boiling water for 15 minutes. When cool, the vegetables are placed in a sterile jar for preservation. Vinegar that has been boiled, simmered, and cooled can be added over the vegetables in the jar. Grape leaves can be picked in early summer and preserved in this manner.

Modern canning will require equipment and knowledge as to the low acid fruits and vegetables that require pressure canning. You must follow instructions to avoid deadly botulism toxin poisoning from a bacteria that grows in the soil. Botulism bacteria is an anaerobe, it does not require oxygen and can multiply in improperly prepared home canned foods. The USDA has a *Guide to Canning* publication that should be studied.

Dehydrating is an easier process using the sun or wind. Fruits and vegetables can be preserved by washing, peeling, removing seeds, slicing and drying in the sun or heat source for 5-8 hours in at least 65 degree heat. Apples, grapes, peaches, tomatoes, beets, potatoes, pumpkin, corn, onions, celery, broccoli, beans, carrots, greens and most other vegetables and fruits can be dehydrated. Some sources describe placing pans of thin sliced fruits on pans on the roof. The food should be flattened and covered with cheesecloth, wax paper or plastic screens to protect them from being eaten or contaminated by birds and insects. Plastic screens are sold where food dehydrators are sold.

Fruits can be jellied with sugar and jarred to inhibit bacteria growth.

A root cellar dug below the frost line can keep root vegetables dormant, but alive, for weeks under leaves. Carrots, cabbage and apples can be kept for months in cold storage. A wood frame can be built inside a cavity in a hillside and enclosed with a door or outdoor vents. A vented enclosure could be constructed in the basement to keep that area colder. Vents can be added in the basement by boring holes though the wall or replacing the windows with plywood and installing vents in the plywood.

What is the best place for storage?

All survival supplies should be stored in a dry and cool condition. The sealed containers of medicine, first aid supplies, ammunition and food can be placed inside new five gallon "paint buckets" with a tight fitting lid or a new metal garbage can with a tight fitting lid. All containers should be labeled and reused for the same type of supplies.

Should you use drying agents?

The lifetime of your food and ammunition supplies will increase by storing them with a desiccant. Silica gel desiccant packets should be placed inside of the storage containers to further avoid oxygen degradation.

Packets of silica gel packets are available for purchase on the internet. Supplies in a five gallon bucket will need a 10 gm silica gel package. Two cubic feet of storage will require 28 grams of silica gel. Our source was silicagelpackets.com.

Canned fish stores easily and will supplement grains

Primitive survival recipes follow in the next chapter.

Chapter Six
Survival Recipes

The following are some primitive American recipes used during the civil war and pioneer days. These recipes require only the grains, salt, fat and water that are part of the survival supplies you will have stored. We encourage you to experiment with these recipes and acquire the ingredients before the emergency. There are many opportunities to add a fresh fruit, or seasoning, to add flavoring.

Primitive cookware like cast iron pans and pots with lids will be necessary for cooking on an open fire. A metal tripod can be used to hang the kettles over the fire. These supplies are available in camping supply stores. For most of the stored food supply you only need to boil water for cooking, so a large pot with a lid for boiling water will be critical.

These primitive recipes were intended to create food that could sustain pioneers or soldiers and did not require refrigeration.

It is a good idea to practice these recipes. If you do not have positive results there are variations on these recipes available in cook books.

Hardtack

2 Cups flour

½ Cup water

1 Tablespoon fat

1 Teaspoon salt

Make a stiff dough, roll to ¼ inch thickness, poke holes and bake half an hour on each side until dry. During the Civil War soldiers were provided nine pieces of hard tack a day. You can use solar or campfire cooking methods described in a later chapter.

Flapjacks

1 cup flour of any ground grain

½ teaspoon salt

1 teaspoon baking powder

Add water till a thin batter is formed. Cook like a pancake on both sides.

Johnny Cake

1 cup cornmeal, (ground, dried corn kernels)

½ teaspoon salt

Add water and mix, form into biscuit or flat cake, and bake 20 minutes in pan until brown.

Matzo crackers

Mix flour and water quickly, spread thin, poke holes, and bake. The flour can be ground oats, wheat, barley or rye.

Sourdough starter

4 cups flour

3 teaspoons sugar

2 teaspoons salt

4 cups water

Put the mix in a container in a warm place and cover for two days.

Use 3/4 of the starter for baking and add equal amounts of flour and water to the remaining ¼ of the starter for your next batch.

We have not experimented with this recipe.

Sourdough bread

1 Tablespoon fat

1 cup flour

1 teaspoon baking powder

Use ¾ of the sourdough starter, prepared above

Mix, knead, put in warm place until it doubles in size and then bake

Primitive bread

Mix about a cup of flour with 1 teaspoon baking powder, and ½ teaspoon of salt, and add water to make dough. Knead the dough and wrap it around a green twig and hold over campfire.

Meat Preservation and Warning

It is likely that the survival diet will consist of plants and grains. If you are provided meat, you may need to preserve it. These are recipes used in the past. We suggest that the final product be refrigerated if possible. A food safety warning follows.

Pemmican

Cut thin strips of lean meat, trimming fat away. Hang the strips of meat over a campfire to smoke for two days until dry and meat splinters and breaks when bent. Pound the smoked and dehydrated meat until almost a powder. Mix meat with dried berries if desired. Add rendered fat (chopped, simmered and strained). Compress the mixture into small air tight packages. It should be very hard. This is the recipe reported to be used by plains Indians. See the food safety warning that follows.

Jerky

Cut thin strips of lean meat into 1/8-1/4" thick pieces and 1" wide. Trim away all fat. Marinate if desired. Lay strips in oven at 150 degrees for 8-12 hours or until thoroughly dry. Meat should break if bent. Store in a sealed air tight jar.

Food Safety Warning

We have not attempted these basic and old pioneer recipes for jerky and pemmican. Meats are a potentially hazardous food that could support dangerous bacteria growth if not properly prepared and stored. Read more detailed instructions and newer recipes that incorporate modern food safety measure before attempting to preserve these meat products. Added steps as salting, seasoning and sugaring will assist with antimicrobial preservation.

Chapter Seven
Wild Edible Plants

If there are more people than you expected sharing your food reserves, the government has confiscated your supply or it has been stolen or destroyed, you will have to forage for food in the wild.

Some people may expect to survive on fresh caught fish, or hunting geese, ducks, deer, squirrels or rabbits. **However, unless you are in a remote location these wild edibles will be exterminated quickly.** Millions of evacuees may be competing for the wild edibles.

Fish supply very few calories, it would be necessary to consume a half dozen fish a day to survive. Hunters have died from eating only lean meat of rabbits. It takes calories to digest food, especially protein.

A variety of foods and oils are necessary for survival. Nuts have a high calorie content and some beneficial oils and are excellent survival supplements.

What do you do when the food supply is depleted?

We will want to enhance the diet with fresh wild plants and fruits in every season. **We will use wild food to supplement our stored food whenever it is available for enhanced nutrition.**

When your stored food is depleted, the first source of gathered food is in a former farmer's fields. The cultivated crops will continue to grow wild for a few seasons. Corn kernels can be eaten raw, roasted, or parched and ground into flour.[81]

> "An EMP attack that disrupts the food infrastructure could pose a threat to life, industrial activity and social order. Absolute deprivation of food, on average, will greatly diminish a person's capacity for physical work within a few days. After 4 to 5 days without food, the average person will suffer from impaired judgment and have difficulty performing simple intellectual tasks. After 2 weeks without food the average person will be virtually incapacitated. Death typically results after 1 or 2 months without food."[82]

Wild plants are edible?

40% of wild plants are edible.

Pine nuts from pine cones, dandelion flowers and leaves, queen anne's lace root, raspberries, apples, and nuts are readily available in the wild.

It is important to buy an edible plant identification book for survival food. Some weeds can cause allergic reactions, especially to those who are sensitive to the ragweed, marigold and the daisy family.

Avoid eating wild plants that taste bitter and generally avoid milky juice plants. Avoid any plants with an almond scent, indicating cyanide. Some plants contain arsenic poison also.

---

[81] Department of the Army Field Manual, Survival, October 1970 p 122

[82] 82 Dr. Foster, John S. Jr, et al, *"Critical National Infrastructures"*, April 2008 p 134

Always follow the rule, "leaves of three, let it be" to prevent poison ivy collection. The lesser known, wild parsnip, resembles queen anne's lace. Instead of white flowers, wild parsnip has greenish/yellow flowers. The juice in the parsnip plant will cause a blistering skin rash.

Even when you have identified a new source of wild plant as edible, first try a small taste and watch for symptoms for a day. Try only one new edible plant a day. If someone should eat a poisonous plant by accident have them drink plenty of water and try to cause vomiting, unless they are unconscious or convulsing

Any edible weed additions to the diet should be used in small quantities to supplement needed vitamins.

What plant parts are edible?

The edible portions of plants can be roasted, ground, made into flour, or used as a fresh salad.

Edible plant parts may be described as:

1. greens- usually the newest and youngest leaves can be eaten raw or cooked

2. shoots- the tender stems of young plants, usually boiled

3. roots and tubers- below soil level and usually dug for in the fall season. They can be cleaned, peeled, and sliced for baking or boiling. They can be stored in a cellar covered with leaves for preparation months later. The dried root can be ground for flour

4. fruits- eat whole and raw if ripe, or bake if green. Press and strain through cheesecloth for juice.

5. grains- the plant can be knocked on a board to remove grain, then the grain manually rubbed to remove the chaff, then milled or ground to produce flour. You may find grains in an abandoned farm field. Crops continue to grow where they were once planted. Some American weeds were cultivated grains in Europe.

6. nuts- can be eaten raw or milled into flour. Boil acorns in several changes of water to remove the tannic acid. Use a hammer to open walnut and other hard husks.

What are examples of edible plants?

The following are examples of common edible plants. If you aren't already thoroughly familiar with these plants in the wild, then you must verify their identity in an edible plant book.

Dandelions have vitamin A, C, potassium and iron. The leaves can be cooked and the flower buds and flowers cooked or fried. The root can be dug up in the late summer and washed and baked and ground for coffee.

Queen anne's lace may be plentiful. The root is actually a wild carrot and should smell like a carrot. Use a field guide for identification, because it resembles poison hemlock. The queen anne's lace has a hairy stem, the primary difference. Poison hemlock grows in wet areas. Also, avoid confusion with the greenish-yellow flowered wild parsnip, that causes a blistering and long lasting rash.

Pigweed (lamb's quarter's) leaves are best eaten after boiling. The seeds can be boiled for cereal or ground into flour. The seeds were once grown by farmers as a grain. It grows three to four feet tall. In late summer, it can be recognized by the tall shoot of green seeds extending up on a spike. The young leaves can be eaten raw and older leaves cooked. It is high in Vitamin C, beta carotene, calcium and iron. The seeds are rich in lysine and Vitamins E and B. In late summer you can collect the seeds to harvest. In some conditions, especially a drought, the plant can accumulate toxic levels of nitrates.

Purslane leaves and stems can be boiled as greens or eaten raw in salads. The tiny black seeds can be made into flour. Henry David Thoreau talked of making dinner of purslane. It resembles a jade plant with thick green oval leaves. The leaves and stems contain iron, Vitamin A and C calcium and phosphorus. Leafy spurge is a poisonous plant that is sometimes confused with purslane. Leafy spurge presents a milky sap when a stem is cracked open.

Chickweed is widespread and rich in vitamins. It blooms small white flowers in early spring. The leaves and stems can be used raw, but are best cooked for 5 minutes and are rich in Vitamin C, Vitamins B6 and B12, potassium, iron and magnesium. Spotted spurge is a poisonous plant that has a similar leaf. Spotted spurge will display a milky sap when broken open.

Chicory leaves can be eaten raw. The root can be roasted and ground for coffee replacement. Chicory grows two to four feet tall on roadsides and has numerous blue flowers in summer.

Wild onions are widespread. The bulb of the onion smells just like an onion. The bulbs can be boiled or eaten raw in salads. The tender leaves can be cooked as greens. It should smell like an onion. If it doesn't, avoid eating it, it may be a similar, but poisonous plant.

Cattail roots can be eaten baked or roasted after peeling and grating. The new shoots can also be eaten. Cattails grow near water in most parts of the country.

What fruits and vines may be edible (or dangerous)?

Wild grapes grow on climbing vines in most parts of the country. The grapes can be crushed and wrung through cheesecloth to obtain the juice. The juice should sit for two days and the sludge at the bottom of the juice container discarded. The grapevine leaves can be stored in salt water in a jar.

(However, moonseed is similar to grape vines but is poisonous. Moonseed has a single crescent shaped seed in the fruit, and has no tendrils on the vines. Consult your edible plant guide.)

In the spring and early summer, you may find fresh strawberries on plants with white flowers. (If you observe an apparent strawberry plant without white flowers, it may not be a strawberry, and it could be poisonous.)

Mulberries, currants, and blackberries can be found in bushes and trees. (The mulberry fruits should only be eaten if ripe).

Elderberry flowers and fruits are edible. (other parts of the elderberry plant are poisonous.)

Apple trees produce a lot of fruit. Green and small apples should be cooked before eating. (Do not eat apple seeds, they contain a cyanide compound.)

Apple vinegar can be produced by placing apple peels and cores in a bucket with warm water, cover with a cloth and place in a warm location for two to six weeks. The liquid below the slime layer should be vinegar.

What about nuts and edible trees?

In the fall and winter, collect nuts from hickory and walnut trees. (Walnuts can harbor parasites so they should be roasted in your campfire or solar oven to destroy the parasites)

Pine nuts can be found in mature pine cones of some species. The mature cones can be bagged and stored in the heat and then pounded to dislodge the nuts. In some species the nuts are too small to make the effort.

Acorn nuts are edible too, but they contain tannin. Boil for two hours and change the water occasionally. You can eat them as nuts or make a paste by mixing the boiled acorns with water, let dry, and then grind into flour.

If desperate, the inner barks of basswood, tamarack, willow, birch, spruce and many pine trees are edible. Avoid the brown bark because it has too much tannin. (Too much tannic acid can cause kidney failure) The edible thin inner bark is white and is between the green lining and the outside bark. Flour can be made of the inner bark of cottonwood, birch, aspen, and willow or pine trees.[83]

The birch and maple trees produce edible sweet sap that can be collected by hammering a hole upward through the bark and nailing a container just below the hole. A friend from Russia describes drinking birch sap immediately after collection in the spring. She describes it as tasting like watermelon juice and plentiful.

Chewing on a spruce needle can provide some Vitamin C. Green pine needle tea can also provide Vitamin C. This is important in winter, or whenever fresh greens are not available to eat.

Are there other concerns with wild plants?

Wild mushrooms should be avoided. If you pick even one poison mushroom in your collection by accident it can contaminate the entire collection. Many poisonous mushrooms look similar to the edible types.

---

[83] Department of the Army Field Guide, <u>Survival,</u> 1970 p108

Raw greens often contain parasites. To kill them, soak the greens in a mild apple cider vinegar solution for 15 minutes. (1 tablespoon vinegar to one gallon of water)

A bitter almond smell in any plant may indicate cyanide. Any plant with this odor should be avoided.

Are there additional sources of food?

1. For additional protein, grubs can be found in the dirt under rotting wood.

2. If you are near a waterway, clams, crawfish, and snails are edible.

3. Frogs can be eaten after the skin is removed. Some secrete an irritating fluid in their skin.

4. Turtles are edible. Do not grab a snapping turtle until you know it is dead.

5. Most dried vegetables that you have sliced and placed covered on pans in the sun to dry, can be ground into flour or boiled in soups.

6. Insects of 1400 species are eaten by humans around the world. The most common insects consumed are beetles, ants, bees, wasps, grasshoppers, crickets, moths and butterflies. The Food and Agriculture Organisation of the United Nations has hosted meetings encouraging the expanded use of insects as food and promoting the protein content. We recommend the insects be roasted or smoked to kill parasites before eating.

What are other survival uses of some wild plants?

Cattail leaves are useful for weaving containers. The leaves can also be dried and burned as an insect repellant.

Dandelion juice and pine tree resin can be used as a glue.

Chapter Eight
Some Poisonous Plants

We highly recommend that you purchase and keep <u>A Field Guide to Edible Wild Plants</u> by Lee Allen Peterson or the U.S. Army <u>Illustrated Guide to Edible Wild Plants</u> in your survival library. <u>The Forager's Harvest</u> by Samuel Thayer is a good practical guide also. Details on these books are included in the recommended reading list in the appendix.

What are examples of poisonous plants?

The following is a partial list of poisonous plants. In some plants, parts are poisonous and other parts are edible. In some cases, the ripe berries are not poisonous, but the remainder of the plant is. The details will be provided in any edible plant guide.

Azalea

Baneberries

Black locust

Blue cohosh

Buckthorns

Buttercups

Butterfly weed

Castor bean

Chokecherry

Clematis

Common tansy

Cowbane

Elderberry

Golden seal

Holly

Horse chestnut

Hydrangea

Jack in the pulpit

Jimsonweed

Kentucky coffee tree

Lantana

Larkspur

Marsh marigold

May apple

Mistletoe

Mushrooms

Nightshades

Poison hemlock

Pokeweed

Rhododendron

Skunk cabbage

Star of Bethlehem

Virginia creeper

Water hemlock

Wild cherries

Chapter Nine
Water

"By disrupting the water infrastructure an EMP attack could pose a major threat to life, industrial activity and social order. Denial of water can cause death in 3 to 4 days, depending on the climate and level of activity."[84]

In the first few hours after the loss of power, the gravity from the municipal water towers will still provide water to homes. The supply will end when the tank is not replenished by the pumps to the tower. In these first hours, fill your bathtubs and any other containers with water. Remember that you will have some supply in the hot water tank also. Swimming pools are another source of water. **Fill every container that you can find**. The water will be used for drinking and food preparation.

Currently, we use 100 gallons of water per person per day. Primitive campers describe using 5 gallons a day for cooking and drinking and 10 gallons a day for bathing and laundry.

A U.S. Army handbook states that we lose a quart of water an hour in severe heat. Only inactivity during the heat will conserve body fluid. The climate, the season and your activity will affect the amount of water you require.

How do you store water?

---

[84] Dr. Foster, John S. Jr, et al, *"Critical National Infrastructures"*, Report of the Commission to Assess the Threat of EMP, April 2008 p 143

In our basement, we have a new plastic 35 gallon tank that we keep pre-filled with water for emergency. We use drops of chlorine to disinfect it and replace the supply every six months. **Before we drink the water we would allow the chlorine to completely evaporate in an open container or dissipate by boiling.** We have chlorine test strips to measure the level of chlorine (bleach). It should not exceed 2-4 parts per million (ppm) to drink. You should not be able to smell or taste the chlorine.

How do you efficiently collect rain water?

Rainwater can be collected using various methods and is a relatively clean source of drinking water. Five gallon plastic paint pails with lids can be purchased at home building supply stores. You should mark these for "water collection only". Paint pail lids have a rubber gasket to make a better seal. The lids are purchased separately from the pail.

Rainwater collection methods:

1. Tarps can be folded into a large funnel to discharge into a pail.
2. The downspout can be cut to flow into a pail.
3. Holes can be strategically placed in an eave and pails placed beneath.

The rainwater should be filtered and disinfected before drinking if it touched any surface. Rain water is safe until it touches the ground, roof or eaves where bird or animal feces are present.

Can a private home well still function?

With the power grid off, getting water from a well will be difficult. A gasoline or propane generator may be able to run a well pump for a few months, but eventually you will run out of fuel. If you buy a generator to run your well make sure it is large enough to start the pump. A deep well may require a 220 volt, high wattage generator.

An alternative, when you no longer have power for your well pump, is to construct a manual water "pail" that will fit inside the well casing. Newer wells range from 50' to 600' deep. The well casing holds about 1 ½ gallons of water per foot and will fill with water up to 25 feet of the surface.

A short PVC pipe with an end cap on the bottom can be used to make a deep narrow "pail" that will fit down the narrow well pipe. Water will flow into the top of the pipe to fill. Add weight to the bottom of the "pail" so it will sink and fill with water. Attach a strong rope to the top of the "pail" long enough to reach the water level in the well. This is something best purchased and made ahead of time as part of your disaster plan. If the well is sufficiently shallow, a hand crank siphon can be used.

If your property is subject to flooding, or you are in a valley, your well is probably shallow. If you are on a hilltop or dry ground, your well is probably deep.

Can you dig your own well like the pioneers?

If your land is in a valley and the soil is not too rocky, you may be able to hand dig a well. You can hammer a series of hollow metal pipes down (if you have the supplies on hand), you can use a hand auger or you can hand dig a wide hole. You should look at detailed well digging methods in preparation.

You may find a natural spring or dried streambed on your property where the water table is just below the ground. Look for dense plant growth or animal trails to a specific site. You can dig into the spring, a hole deep enough to scoop your water pail for collection.

Mechanical windmills were built directly on top of hand dug wells in the past to pump water.

"Demoralization and deterioration of social order can be expected to deepen if a water shortage is protracted. Anarchy will certainly loom if government cannot supply the population with enough water to preserve health and life."[85]

What other sources of water could be used?

First, use all the stored water in the home. The hot water heater, sump pumps and toilet tanks are some sources.

Clothes washing, body washing and shampooing will probably be done during rain storms outdoors if the water shortage is critical. Hanging clothes in the sun outdoors daily will allow some disinfection without water.

The water in the footing drain sump pump will be repeatedly refilled if there is sufficient supply from rain. It should be filtered and disinfected with chlorine or boiled to destroy bacteria.

---

[85] Dr. Foster, John S. Jr, et al, *"Critical National Infrastructures"*, April 2008 p 144

Snow and ice can be melted and purified. Do not eat snow or ice without melting because it will reduce your body temperature, leading to dehydration.

You can collect dew on the grass in the morning with a cloth which can be wrung into a container also. This would be a good source of water for cleaning rags.

How do you purify water that you collect?

Prior to disinfecting the water for drinking, you should first filter out the sediment. Filter large particles out by pouring the water through a coffee filter, cotton, or cheesecloth fabric. You can also use a water filter pitcher. The more particles in the water, the higher the concentration of added chlorine that is necessary because the chlorine will be degraded by the process of disinfecting the particles. This is why filtering is important.

Water can be purified by boiling for five minutes or chemically treating with chlorine (bleach). Make certain the household bleach contains sodium hypochlorite and not added fragrances or chemicals. Longer boiling will kill hardier organisms. The boiling will reduce the oxygen in the water and it will taste flat. To add oxygen, simply pour the water back and forth between two clean containers.

To purify water with household liquid bleach (sodium hypochlorite) premixed and purchased from the store, just add 8 drops to each gallon of water and test the concentration with chlorine test strips. Read and follow the label directions on the container for purifying water if they differ from the above. Always read and follow precautions on the labels. Household bleach degrades over time.

In order to store a large amount of chlorine disinfectant for long periods of time, many survivalists prefer to use dry chlorine as calcium hypochlorite. It is known as "pool shock" at retail stores. Make certain the pool shock contains calcium hypochlorite only and not additional chemicals. Sometimes algae control chemicals are added and you do not want to drink added chemicals.

When preparing the solution add the pool shock granules to the water, do not add water to the pool shock. Store the calcium hypochlorite in a cool dry location away from a heat source. Read the label directions for precautions.

Mixing the granulated pool shock solution will require a **two step** process.

First, to dilute the approximate 70% chlorine content in pool shock to the level of ordinary liquid bleach at 5-6% chlorine.

Step One- Add and mix 1 oz. of the dry calcium hypochlorite to 14 oz. of water to dilute the concentration to about 5%. (A gallon of water is 128 ounces.)

Second, to add the diluted mix into the water to be purified. You will need to have several measuring cups.

Step Two- Add 8 drops of the diluted chlorine mix from above, (or add 8 drops of liquid bleach) to each gallon of water and wait 30 minutes for the antibacterial action. The 8 drops of diluted (5%) chlorine should provide 4 ppm of chlorine per gallon.

4 ppm is the maximum allowable chlorine content in drinking water.

If you are treating water from a stagnant pond you should let it stand for a week if possible. You may have to test and replenish the chlorine each day.

One study found that chlorine killed Hepatitis A virus in about 15 minutes, but Cryptosporidium, another water borne illness, took six days to be killed. Depending on the source of the water, long term disinfection may be necessary. As added protection, we will probably treat drinking water by boiling and with chlorine.

How do you avoid drinking the chlorine?

It is a good idea to buy a pool test kit or test strips (0-200 ppm strips) for detecting chlorine.

The maximum allowed amount of chlorine in drinking water is 4 parts per million (ppm) or 4 milligrams per liter. However, the recommended residual amount of chlorine is 2 ppm.

If you run out of your chlorine test strips, all of the smell and taste of chlorine should be evaporated before drinking. If not, heat the water and wait until you can no longer smell or taste the bleach before drinking. Chlorine will be degraded by sunlight and evaporates in heat.

Are there dangers in using chlorine?

Toxic levels of chlorine could dissolve the mucus membranes and can cause respiratory injury and death.

Chlorine should not be mixed with acid because it will create an unstable chlorine gas. Chlorine becomes toxic when mixed with ammonia which has caused the death of housewives who mixed ordinary household cleaners. Remember that ammonia is a component of urine and some floor and window cleaners. Chlorine is heavier than air and vapors from a spill will concentrate near the floor.

You will want to store the bleach or pool shock in a safe, dry and well ventilated area. Do not store it near the batteries.

What about water contamination?

Surface water sources, especially if stagnant, will pose a risk of chemical and bacterial contamination. It is better to use water below the ground. Undisturbed soil is a remarkable bacteria and chemical filter. **In many soil types, a perched water table will be present within three feet of the surface.** The perched water table is where a season of rain filtered down to an impermeable layer of rock and is trapped. It can be acquired by digging a few feet below the ground after a rainstorm and pressing and scooping the water out. Make certain that where you dig for water is about a hundred horizontal feet from a septic field or where you are burying wastes.

The ground water will need to be filtered and disinfected in the same manner as the rain water.

If you must take water from a surface source, choose a wild, fast running stream, waterfall or river. The action of rocks, sunlight and oxygen will have some antimicrobial effect.

Are there water purifiers available to purchase?

Water filters are constructed of three types, ceramic filters, activated carbon filters or glass fiber filters. Some of the filters are impregnated with a chemical antibacterial treatment also.

There are some filter manufacturers that report that they filter out disease causing bacteria. If you want to purchase these systems for filtering, carefully study their range of products and the types of organisms that will be filtered out of the water. One filter claims to even filter viruses.

Two examples of water filters that claim to filter pathogenic bacteria are the Berkey Water Filter™ and the X-Pack water filter.

The Big Berkey Water Filter™, available at (www.bigberkeywaterfilters.com), uses gravity, so no electrical power is needed. Two Berkey filters will last a year if you purify 3 gallons a day.

The X-Pack water filter (www.xpackprepared.com) was reportedly used during Hurricane Katrina to drink surface water. The filter used in the X-Pack is only good for 10 days. This is an expensive option for an extended survival situation. However, this is a useful item for an emergency backpack.

To insure the maximum life for water filters, be sure to remove any large particles before using the filter. Letting sediments drop to the bottom and pre-filtering through a cloth or coffee filter will eliminate larger particles.

Chapter Ten
Communications

Communications are critical for survival. At some point in time you will need to transmit messages for help or to contact family or friends. You will want redundant methods of communication because of the potential EMP damage to transmission equipment. The cell phone or land phone may work until the battery back up has been depleted, but do not count on it. Further options for communication are discussed in this chapter.

> "an EMP attack would disrupt or damage a functionally significant fraction of the electronic circuits in the Nation's civilian telecommunications systems in the region exposed to EMP."[86]
>
> "Cellular networks are seen as being less robust to EMP than landline networks due to a combination of the higher susceptibility of cellular network equipment to damage and more limited backup power capacity at cell sites than at counterpart landline network equipment sites."[87]

[86] Dr. Foster, John S Jr, "Critical National Infrastructures," p 150

[87] Dr. Foster, John S. Jr, et al, "Critical National Infrastructures", April 2008   p 68

> "To offset a loss of electric power, telecommunication sites now use a mix of batteries mobile generators and fixed location generators. Typically these have 4 to 72 hours of backup power available on site and thus will depend on either the resumption of electrical utility power or fuel deliveries to function for longer periods of time."[88]

How do you communicate with friends after the phone and cell phones quit functioning?

An amateur radio transceiver is the second line of communication. You can contact friends and family if they know what frequency and time you will be transmitting.

As with all electronics, they must be stored in advance in improvised "faraday cages", to protect them from damage from the EMP. At a minimum, the antenna should be removed and appliances disconnected from outdoor antenna if you plan on using them after an EMP.

Yaesu FT-817ND

---

[88] Dr. Foster, John S. Jr, et al, *"Critical National Infrastructures"*, April 2008 p 68

Amateur (Ham Radios), will provide short or long distance communication with other ham radio operators. Battery operated and low power equipment will be needed in a power grid emergency. Amateur radios will allow you to speak directly to other operators potentially in other parts of the world to assess the extent of the disaster.

Amateur radio licenses are available from the FCC after testing, based on a home study course. The ARRL is the national association for Amateur Radio. The technician license is earned after passing a 35 question FCC exam. Study materials are available from ARRL, www.arrl.org or 1-800-new-ham (326-3942).

Amateur radio operators are trained to provide assistance in national emergencies. It is possible it will be the only method of personal communication. Amateur radio clubs across the country practice "field days" emergency communication practices each year.

Our recommended amateur radio units, based on low power requirements, are the ICOM®-703 or Yaesu-FT817ND. You can visit the company websites at www.icomamerica.com or www.yaesu.com for more information.

If you have sufficient electrical power available, a Yaesu-450AT or ICOM® IC-718 will provide more communication power. Amateur radio operators will also need an independent source of power. All power operated communication will cease working when the batteries are depleted.

A solar panel that charges a 12 volt battery can be used to recharge smaller batteries allowing continued communication in your home base and retreat location with battery powered equipment.

We anticipate that amateur radio operators will post text messages at fire or police stations to link messages between families and friends.

Is there any other method of getting news immediately?

Police scanners, shortwave radios and CB radios, if battery powered and protected from an EMP pulse, can provide communication.

 A police scanner is essential equipment to obtain local emergency information. The scanner must be stored, in advance, in a faraday cage to insure it will work after an EMP.

Each county has their own police and emergency frequencies. You can obtain this information on the internet now and pre-program it into your scanner. You should program in every frequency of every county you will travel through if you will be traveling to a remote location. Radio Shack® has been a good source for police scanners and rechargeable batteries in our preparations.

A battery operated police scanner may answer the following:

What is the traffic situation and evacuation route?

What is the enforcement plan of the government?

What clues are there as to the cause of the outage?

Are there emergency shelters?

Is the government confiscating survival supplies?

Is there crime activity in the local area?

Are foreign military forces present?

Shortwave radio receivers are widespread in third world countries, but not in the U.S. Shortwave transmissions travel much farther than broadcast, but depend on atmospheric conditions. Voice of America® and BBC© World Service broadcast to shortwave receivers. A shortwave radio can be used to communicate internationally to learn news and advise you of the following:

What is the scale of the power outage?

How far away is safety?

Is any government working on remedying the outage and when may it be completed?

Are there disease epidemics?

Are foreign military forces being sent for humanitarian efforts?

For local communication in the neighborhood or town, **CB radios are useful.**

The CB radio can be used to communicate on neighborhood patrols. You could provide one of your units to a friendly neighbor who is assisting with food gathering or patrolling. However, if you are trying to remain isolated in a dangerous environment, you will not want to use the CB because there are scanning listening devices that can locate your position.

A CB radio comes in a few varieties;

1. The AM types are inexpensive but require a lot of power. They can also be heard by others.

2. The SSB (single side band) CB radios have a longer range and require less power. They are less likely to be heard by outsiders. Their range is from 5 to 15 miles.

You should agree on what channel to use in advance.

What if you want to be found in an emergency?

On occasion you may want outsiders to assist you in an emergency. If you are at a distance from help you can signal for assistance to anyone who can see the SOS call for help, with a flashlight. Three short flashes, three longer flashes, and three short flashes again, signals SOS. You can improvise a flashlight by shading a lantern with a cloth or cardboard to simulate the signal.

Because of the security issue of looters who may be watching for inhabitants and provisions, you should pre-arrange a signal pattern with neighbors. During the day, if you want to signal neighbors, you can also hang "flags" in a high tree. The flags could be pre-arranged as plastic grocery bags, or other common wind blown objects, that looters would not necessarily recognize as a signal of occupancy.

You could also use a signal mirror by employing sunlight and a shiny surface to reflect the sunlight and call attention to your need for emergency help.

Three is an emergency signal. Three gunshots, three whistle blasts or three smoky fires should be recognized as an emergency signal.

Chapter Eleven
Faraday Cages

If you want to use battery operated electronics during the outage or to protect your power devices from EMP damage, you must build "faraday cages".

The faraday cage is named after an electricity experimenter and inventor, Michael Faraday, who coated a room with metal foil in 1836 and blasted the exterior of the room with electricity and found the electric charge was absent inside the room.

How can you make a faraday cage for each of your electronics?

You can create your own faraday cage using these options:

1. You can put two cardboard boxes inside each other and the electronic device inside the smallest. The outer box would be covered with overlapping aluminum foil, and taped securely.

2. You can cover the electronics with a Mylar sheet (space blanket). This is a good option for heavy or permanently positioned equipment. You would want to unplug the appliances and remove any antenna.

3. You can line a metal box with plastic and keep the electronic device inside of the plastic insulation. We purchased metal tins

with metal lids, of several sizes from a variety store. We purchased foam from a fabric store to line the inside of the tins.

4. You can insulate the inside of a new metal garbage can with foam or plastic and cover with a tight fitting lid.

5. You can buy flat metallic shielding bags. 4X6 inch bags cost $8 for 100. 20X24 inch bags cost $80 from www. global industrial.com. These are sometimes called EMP bags. These protect against static electricity. We will use these in combination with another shield.

6. You can buy a shielding system from Holland Shielding Systems, LBA Group Inc, or 3M Corp. They have information available on the internet.

Some sources say you should add a ground wire from the cage, other sources say no. The problem with a ground wire is that it may act as an antenna and increase the risk of EMP damage. We chose not to add a ground wire.

To protect your electronics you should keep them unplugged, with the antenna lowered. The faraday cage must be in place before the EMP event. After an EMP event, it is no longer necessary unless you anticipate another attack.

How can you protect electronic data?

An EMP attack will probably disable computers and destroy data stored in the computers. Computers are particularly vulnerable because of the sophisticated electronics and wires connecting the computer to a network and peripheral equipment. The wires act as an antenna to pick up and magnify the EMP pulse.

The electronics in hard drives will be fried from the EMP, making the drive inoperative. Data stored on DVD, CD-Rom or USB/Thumb/Flash drive may still be intact, but inaccessible without a working computer. An EMP of 100kV/m may be high enough to destroy electronic parts that are not plugged into the grid.

How do you protect important documents?

The first level of protection is to keep paper copies of important documents. Keep paper copies of all financial records. Make sure you have paper copies of the title for your house, cars, and other important items you own. You may need to prove ownership if squatters take over your residence.

Don't depend on the government having good records. Even if the government is intact, their files have probably been destroyed. The military has been actively protecting their equipment against EMP but the civilian government has not.

Next, keep a copy of your important files in a protected external drive. Buy a small external drive that plugs into a USB port on your computer. Back up your important files on a regular schedule. Disconnect all cables from the drive and store it in a small faraday cage.

Another idea is to save an old notebook PC that may be slow but still functions. Disconnect all cables and store your old PC in a faraday cage. If disaster strikes, you will have your important files backed up and have a computer to read them, possibly years later. As a further step, you may want to protect an old printer (and ink cartridge) in a faraday cage so you can print your documents at a later time when power is restored.

What items should be stored in a faraday cage now?

1. Emergency Radio
2. Police scanner
3. CB radio
4. Backup solar panels (wrap in foil)
5. Backup battery conditioner for solar panels
6. Backup charger for rechargeable batteries
7. Backup wind power electronics
8. Backup hard drive with computer files
9. Backup notebook computer
10. Amateur radios
11. Backup 115 volt inverter
12. iPod for music
13. Extra fuses for all electronics

Chapter Twelve
Solar, Wind and Fire Power

Solar and wind energy are likely to be the only sources of energy that can be produced after the EMP event. **Solar or wind recharged battery power may need to provide energy needs for a year or longer.** Deep cycle batteries should have the capacity to store three to seven days worth of power at all times, if possible.

This section will describe and quantify the minimum requirements for solar recharging and batteries to run essential power needs for lighting, heat, communication and cooking.

Wind power equipment needs will be addressed and compared to the solar power option.

Propane, firewood, candle and charcoal are also survival fuel options and will be discussed.

> "The petroleum and natural gas infrastructures are critically dependent on the availability of assured electric power from the national grid, as well as all the other critical national infrastructures…" [89]
>
> "In turn, all these infrastructures rely on the availability of fuels provided by the petroleum and natural gas sector"… "But outages of a few days or more can be expected to severely affect all infrastructure operations."[90]

---

[89] Dr. Foster, John S. Jr, et al, "*Critical National Infrastructures*", April 2008 p 103

[90] Dr. Foster, John S. Jr, et al, "*Critical National Infrastructures*", April 2008 p 103

Won't there be other fuel sources like natural gas?

During the Y2K preparation in 1999, people planned on gasoline or natural gas. However, during a power grid failure, gasoline is not available because there is no power for the pumps or electronics that control the pipelines or to refuel tankers.

The electronic SCADA systems of our underground pipeline monitoring and control systems will be damaged by the EMP. Loss of control of underground pipelines could be an issue of public safety.

The retail supply of propane tank fuel in 20 pound tanks and for those in rural properties, in 500 gallon tanks, will need retrofitting for small heating and cooking equipment. You should contact a professional for advice.

Our solar panels purchased from Harbor Freight Tools

How do you start preparing for solar power?

Solar energy will provide backup power for basic lighting and communication. Solar panels are available most often in 12, 24 or 36 volt charges. **For our minimal survival needs 12 volt will be sufficient.** The solar panels will be largely maintenance free except for cleaning and possible waterproofing on the edges. They lose efficiency in hot conditions so you should allow sufficient ventilation to cool the backside of the panels. A solar powered system for essential needs to recharge batteries can be prepared for less than $500.

The best time to purchase an inexpensive solar system back up is now. We found complete solar systems with battery chargers and small panels are available from Harbor Freight Tools www.harborfreight.com and at home building supply retailers like Menards® and Home Depot.®

How do you store solar power?

The solar panels will be used to recharge a deep cycle battery. (deep cycle batteries are detailed later) The battery is then used to power lights and DC powered communication equipment and to recharge the variety of rechargeable batteries for small appliances.

In order to minimize energy usage, newer, low power devices should be purchased. LED lights take much less power than other lights. We already installed LED lights and the wiring from the deep cell battery to the light fixtures in our living area. Newer communication equipment is designed for battery power.

Essential devices are:

1. a few LED lights,
2. a DC powered AM/FM radio,
3. a battery operated, low power shortwave radio for world news,
4. a battery powered, low power police scanner,
5. a battery powered amateur radio,
6. a CB radio for communication with neighbors nearby.

Rechargeable batteries for small devices have a shelf life of four years or less. Plan to replace your batteries every four years. Make sure batteries are kept charged for maximum life. Ideally you should have many rechargeable batteries of standard sizes.

How do you determine how much power you can store?

A simple 12 volt solar panel system will provide solar energy for our essential power needs. To determine your power needs follow the following formula.

First, find out the average hours of sunlight in your geographic area, consult the internet or a text like Solar Living Source Book. (book details are in the appendix)

You should determine what devices you need to power and for how long and then total the wattage for each device.

The total wattage needed should be multiplied by the number of hours of sunlight per day to determine the solar panel size. According to the following table, a solar panel of 45 watts will be sufficient, based on 19 hours of sunlight per week at our retreat home (119 x 7 / 19 = 44).

Device Type	Hours per day	Device power	Watt-hours per day
Three 5 watt LED lights	4	15 watts	60 watt-hours
AM/FM/Short Wave Radio	10	2 watts	20 watt-hours
CB or HAM radio	1	12 watts	12 watt-hours
4 AA battery charging for flashlights and police scanner	0.25	96 watts	24 watt-hours
Apple iPod charging	0.5	6 watts	3 watt-hours
		TOTAL	119 watt-hours

A margin of safety should be added by increasing the watt-hours for battery losses and wiring losses. We purchased two 45 watt solar panels. The 12 volt deep cycle battery bank should be large enough to store three to seven days without sunshine. If more than one battery is used to store energy, it is called a battery bank. (battery banks will be detailed later).

We increased our total requirement to 140 watt hours per day, for expected wiring losses. For seven days, the battery must provide 980 watt hours of power.

(7days x 140 watts with margin of safety = 980 watt hours).

However, batteries are rated in amp hours not watt hours, so we divided 980 watt hours by 12 volts to get amp-hours.

An 82 amp hour deep cycle battery will meet our requirements

(980/12=82 amp hours).

It is a good idea to buy a backup solar system and more deep cycle batteries. The backup could be used in case of battery failure, battery conditioner failure, damage or theft of the solar panels. Another reason for a back up solar system is to charge a battery used specifically for portable power tools or other critical devices.

Will solar panels be at risk of theft or confiscation?

We recommend the solar panels be displayed as inconspicuously as possible. Solar panels displayed on a roof or open field may be an invitation to thieves.

The solar panels can be mounted on a pole or roof, but should not be too obvious. They work near the ground if the sun is not blocked. Newer solar panels are not affected as dramatically as older panels if a portion is shaded. It may be a better solution to cut down vegetation blocking the sun and protect the solar panels from view, near the ground.

After purchase, the solar panel system should be installed temporarily, and then tested to make certain it is operating. If it works, then store it safely away inside until it is needed to minimize theft and damage.

Solar panels may be damaged by an EMP pulse if left outside and exposed. The panels should be stored wrapped with insulation then covered with aluminum foil, to protect against an EMP attack. You may want to install "sacrificial" outside solar panels now to keep your batteries charged. If the panels survive the attack you will have double the power; if not, you will still have the stored solar panels.

What are solar battery chargers?

You can buy solar power battery chargers for AAA, AA, C, and D rechargeable batteries. These make great backup units that will function independent from your large solar panel system. These are small units that can be stored in a Faraday cage for protection from an EMP pulse. They will also make valuable trade items. Buy several of these. They are very economical, selling for about $20. You must monitor the batteries and disconnect them from the charger at the appropriate time because there is no charge controller on these units.

What is a battery bank?

Alternative energy will require energy stored in a battery or more likely, a bank of batteries, with charge controllers and perhaps an inverter.

The battery bank can be connected in series or parallel, or a combination. The battery interconnects are cables attaching the batteries. A thorough study of your battery needs and battery safety issues and consultation with a professional should be conducted before building your battery bank.

An interface box for the wires from the solar panel to the battery could be installed now into the house. The battery would be stored inside the house to prevent freezing but within 40 feet of the panels.

The wiring should be proper gauge wire and shielded from the EMP. 12 Volt and 12 gauge house wiring were installed in our home to the emergency LED lights and radios. Check with a professional for recommendations.

What is a battery charge controller?

A basic battery charger may not automatically monitor the charge and often overcharged the batteries when they were not unplugged at the appropriate time. This can create a safety hazard and reduce the lifespan of the battery. Do not buy a basic battery charger unless you plan on monitoring the charging operation.

It is better to use a battery conditioner or smart charger that is designed to not overcharge the battery.

Batteries require maintenance of temperature and maintenance of normal charge. A charge controller can be placed between the battery bank and the solar panels or wind turbine to prevent overcharging.

There are simple controllers that shut off and restart the charging of the batteries and there are complicated systems that even monitor the battery temperature.

What is a battery conditioner?

The battery conditioner is a computerized device that charges the battery and maintains and prevents sulfation. Sulfation is caused by repeated swings from discharging to charging. You can purchase either a battery charge controller or a battery conditioner. Consult the manufacturer's description for the appropriate device.

Why would you need a battery inverter?

The power in the batteries is DC. Make certain that you have a DC adapter for the equipment and the computers you will use. The power you use regularly in your home is AC, not DC. There are inverters available to convert the power from DC to AC. Buy an inverter that will handle the wattage of the equipment you will want to power.

You can draw several hundred watts from the battery for a short time. However, overuse of AC devices will quickly drain the battery. You may need to judiciously use high wattage devices when there is a lot of sunshine to charge your battery

What is a deep cycle battery?

Deep cycle batteries are best because they are designed to be charged and then discharged through hundreds of cycles. The deep cycle batteries should last five to ten years and are available in 2, 4, 6, or 12 volts as DC power. Battery inactivity, freezing or excess heat can reduce the life expectancy.

The batteries range from 10 pounds to 200 pounds and the size and weight will indicate the amp hours of storage. They are labeled by the number of hours to discharge with a one amp load. A C20 battery will discharge in 20 hours with a 1 amp load (i.e. 12 watt, 12 volt LED light).

The deep cycle batteries are of three types; Flooded Lead Acid (FLA), Sealed AGM, or Sealed Gel Cell. The FLA type lasts the longest if it is maintained by monitoring and refilling with distilled water, as necessary, and removing the sulfate crystals, if they accumulate on the lead plates. Gel cell batteries charge at a slower rate.

AGM batteries are twice the expense, but are safe against leakage and hydrogen fumes that may occur in an FLA.

Deep cycle batteries should never discharge below 20%, a low voltage warning light should be part of your system design. This will increase life expectancy of the battery. Deep cycle batteries should not be overcharged either. Battery chargers with voltage regulation should be used to assure long life.

A nominal 12 voltage deep cycle battery is fully charged at 12.8 volts with no load. When the voltage drops to 12 volts the battery is less than half charged. Keep the battery at least half charged to maximize battery life.

The list of websites in the appendix includes several battery information websites for alternative energy needs.

The entire system will include the solar panels or wind turbine, a charge controller, the battery or bank of batteries and then an inverter if you need AC power instead of DC power.

Could a battery be dangerous?

The battery storage area should be vented to the outside. An overcharged battery can release hydrogen gas.

Baking soda will neutralize spilled lead acid battery electrolyte, vinegar neutralizes spilled NiCad and NiFe battery electrolytes. The appropriate neutralizers should be stored near the batteries. Soap and water should be available in case of battery acid spill on skin or clothing.

You should be cautious about working with metal or wearing metal near the batteries due to short circuit and explosion potential. A disconnect switch and circuit breaker or fuses should be installed to prevent overheating.

It is best to consult an electrical professional for your alternative energy backup system plan. You should first familiarize yourself about alternative energy. You will need the technical knowledge in the future when there is no longer assistance available. A book that details alternative energy preparation is <u>Living Off the Grid: a Simple Guide to Creating and Maintaining a Self-Reliant Supply of Energy, Water, Shelter, and More</u>, by David S. Black. (details in the appendix)

What about wind power?

An alternative to solar power is wind power. Wind power is a better alternative than solar if the sun is blocked by volcanic dust or nuclear winter, in an alternative disaster contingency. Micro wind turbines that produce 20-500 watts are available to re-charge batteries. Most wind turbine manufacturers base their energy production on a 24 mph wind. Wind is strongest in winter. Wind speed must exceed 8 mph in order to produce any energy in most systems.

The greater the height of the rotor and the longer the sweep of the blades increase energy production. Wind turbines should be a minimum of 30' above obstacles within 300 feet so that wind is not blocked. Air density also is a factor, desirable denser air is found at low altitudes and low temperatures.

The key factor in energy production is the average wind speed. You can find information on wind speed in your state at www.windpoweringamerica.gov, or call your local airport for their average wind speed. Wind damage to evergreens is also an indicator.

Wind systems are not as maintenance free as solar power systems and may require climbing and repairing of moving parts. A lightning arrestor should be placed between the turbine and the battery.

Another consideration is that wind generators have electronic parts that may be vulnerable to an EMP attack. You will want to purchase a spare set of electronics as a backup.

The wind turbines should not be attached to a roof because of the potential damaging affect on the structure.

We visited some homes with both solar and wind energy systems and the owners admitted to less maintenance and more energy from the solar systems. However, the wind energy could be an important complement to solar energy based on weather and atmospheric conditions. Some properties are perfectly suited to wind energy.

The SunForce 44444 Wind Generator is small and relatively inexpensive. It produces 12-volt 400-watt maximum energy. The cost is about $500. Less than 8 mph wind provides no energy generation. To achieve the 400 watt maximum energy output a steady 28 mph wind is necessary (a high wind). There is a 30' tower kit available from SunForce for about $400. You can see their product line at www.sunforceproducts.com.

The wind power alternative is not a cost effective option unless you are in a high wind environment. Many residential locations may have zoning restrictions that will limit the use of wind power.

Many complete small wind power systems retail for about $2500. Trenching the 300' distance to the house and the minimum 30' towers increase the cost.

If you have a good location for a wind turbine and want to attempt to build a turbine, a thorough text on creating wind energy is <u>Homebrew Wind Power</u> by Dan Bartmann and Dan Fink. (book details are in the recommended reading list in the appendix)

What about human power generators?

Bicycle and hand generators provide back up power and exercise. Pedaling a bicycle will generate about 65 watts of power. You will need to pedal two hours a day to power basic lights and electronic equipment. A hand generator has less output and would require about four hours a day.

A human power generator should be set up to charge a 12 volt battery. A battery conditioner is needed to provide the correct voltage and protect the battery.

The web site www.windstreampower.com sells human power generators for $550. These are designed to work with 12 volt batteries. If you don't mind the exercise, a human power generator may be a good backup for a solar panel. However, you should plan on doing a lot of pedaling on cloudy days.

Chapter Thirteen
Propane for Heating

Propane fuel can be stored long term and is therefore ideal for heating. Four grill-sized, 20 pound propane cylinders will be needed to provide minimal essential heating of a small basement room for one winter. Each of these 20 pound tanks will hold over four gallons of liquid propane. Fire authorities caution against storing extra propane in a home or garage. Some grills have storage racks underneath for extra outdoor cylinder storage.

Coleman™ Blackcat Catalytic Heater

Basements maintain about 50 degrees, even without heat. In the winter, for maximum efficiency, a small room can be separated in the basement to be heated.

Can I use propane heat indoors?

The Coleman™ Blackcat catalytic heater reportedly can be safely used indoors and produces 3000 BTU. It is sufficient to heat a small room or tent. Read the manufacturer's guidelines for venting.

How much propane will you need?

The heater will run seven hours on one pound of propane. A twenty pound propane cylinder will provide 5 days of 24 hour heat or 15 nights of heat.

Read the manufacturer's instructions and precautions about potentially adapting any propane equipment for a 20 pound cylinder

Four of the 20 pound cylinders will provide 60 nights of heat, the coldest part of winter. If you are using propane for cooking you will need several additional tanks.

A 500 gallon tank stores over 900 pounds of propane. That is over forty-five 20 pound cylinders of propane. A tank that is half full will supply enough propane for a catalytic heater for a room for a winter season.

If you live in a rural environment that allows propane tanks and have a propane furnace or hot water heater, you may have a 500 gallon propane tank. Keep the tank at least 2/3 full to be prepared for emergencies.

Your propane appliances may not work if there is a power grid failure, but the propane fuel may be used for survival heat and cooking. Make sure you have the correct adapters, hose and pressure reducers if you plan to connect existing household equipment to a small heater. Contact a professional for advice in advance.

Propane can be stored for many years

Chapter Fourteen
Cooking Power

If there is sufficient wood within a safe walking distance from your home or retreat, a wood stove is an excellent option. The wood stove can be used for heating and cooking.

Sufficient venting will be required. Professional advice and advance planning and materials to install a fire proof, efficient vent will be necessary. Remember, any fuel based fire will create dangerous levels of carbon monoxide in half an hour. Carbon monoxide is odorless and deadly and the reason you must have expert attention to the ventilation if you cook indoors.

What about outdoor campfires?

To start an emergency fire outdoors, one frequent suggestion is to put rocks in two rows to create a trench and start the kindling between the rows. The wood for the fire should be stepped up from kindling to branches and then to logs. The fire can be pushed to one end of the trench for boiling and cooking on the hot coals.

To start a fire, waterproof matches, a magnesium stick with a steel striker or flint and a striker are convenient options.

It is best to dry wood for a year before using it for a fire. When that is not practical, white ash wood will light quickly even when green. Trees on a ridge will burn better than those in a swamp. Oak, ash, birch, maple hickory, apple and locust trees will burn better than other varieties. Be careful if using evergreen branches or logs because it will throw sparks because of the resin content.

Tent Stove

Wood burning tent stoves are small and light weight for heating and cooking outdoors. Read the manufacturers instructions for safety precautions.

Candle Power

Candles can be used for light cooking as well as lighting. We purchased a supply of emergency 10 hour candles. They produce little light or heat but did last more than 10 hours. Small glass candle holders must be used to retain the wax for longer burning time. We tried to boil 2 cups of water in a saucepan over 4 short party votives candles. After 20 minutes the water was heated to 113 degrees. We tried the same experiment with 4 longer dinner candles. Two cups of water reached 170 degrees in 20 minutes but the candles were burned about 25%. **Candles may be good for heating tea, but are not good for boiling.**

Charcoal for cooking

Charcoal is readily available and a convenient fuel for outdoor cooking. A smaller charcoal grill is best since it will use less charcoal. The grill should have vents that can be tightly closed so that the unused charcoal can be saved. Always use a charcoal grill outdoors.

Charcoal must be stored in a dry area to maintain its usefulness. Double seal the bags in plastic, then store the charcoal in airtight garbage cans. Add silica gel desiccant packets to the can to keep the contents dry. If you use charcoal for everyday grilling, maintaining a large cache may be an economical way to prepare for emergencies. We decided that charcoal is our best cooking fuel option for our suburban home.

Box Oven

Charcoal can be used outdoors in a Box Oven to bake food using only 10 charcoal briquettes. There are many variations for this simple oven design. This is basically a heavy cardboard box insulated with aluminum foil. The box oven is used outdoors on level ground. The foil covered box is placed over a metal rack supported by four cans. The briquettes are placed under the metal rack. The inside of the box should heat to 350 degrees with 10 briquettes. Each additional briquette should add 35 degrees.

Tin Can Oven

The empty cans of soup or large #10 size empty cans can be used as simple stoves. A hole is placed in a section of the bottom of the can to insert and light twigs or candles. Another hole is punched near the top of the can for venting. The food is placed on top of the can to cook.

Dutch Oven

Set a cast iron pot part buried in hot ashes and coals and cover with metal lid. Move more ashes on top of cast iron pot.

Starting Charcoal and Wood Fires

You may need to start a wood or charcoal fire once or twice a day for cooking or heating. A charcoal chimney will make this easy and does not require starter fluid. You can buy a charcoal chimney where grills are sold. You can also create a charcoal chimney with an empty food can with ends removed and ventilation holes punched through. A few sheets of newspaper placed inside the chimney at the base will set the briquettes inside on fire. Remember to store newspapers for this purpose.

Fire starter squares are ideal for charcoal grills, campfires, fireplaces, woodstoves, and pellet and corn stoves. These will burn for 8 to 12 minutes. Remember that when your stored supply of pellets is depleted, there will be no more.

Solar Cooking

Solar cooking is a great way to cook without electricity and uses no precious fuel. Solar cooking requires a sunny day and is most successful from 10 AM to 2 PM. In our experiments this was plenty of time to cook a pot of rice or beans and vegetables.

The web site www.solar-cook.com is a great source of information on solar cooking. You can order several varieties of solar cookers on this site.

 We used the Global Box Sun Oven®, available from www.solar-cook.com, to cook two quart meals in about three hours. This oven acts like a crock pot slow cooker and can make some delicious meals. This is a best selling solar cooker. The temperature reached over 300 degrees and successfully cooked a pot of beans and a pot of rice.

Parabolic solar cookers are best for boiling water.
They focus all of the sun's energy on the cooking pot
suspended in the center of a large dish. They require
supervision because they get very hot quickly. Wind can
be a problem with the large dish. The dish needs to be
moved to follow the sun.

The web site www.solarcooking.org/plans/windshield-
cooker.htm describes how to make a solar funnel cooker
out of a reflective-folding car sunshade, a wire frame grill
rack, and a plastic baking bag.

You should have several solar cookers for cooking and
heating water. A good quality solar oven such as the
Global Box Sun Oven® on the previous page will serve as
our primary solar oven.

You can make your own solar oven using inexpensive
materials. The ovens you make will be great trading
items. We created a small solar oven out of a wooden
frame and thin plastic fresnel lens sheets. Inside, we
placed black-painted pint sized canning jars into a metal
loaf baking pan. We successfully cooked wheat inside the
canning jars on a 25 degree winter day where the oven
reached 200 degrees. Details of our homemade oven are
available in Appendix G, in the back of this book.

Butane Cooking

Small butane cooking stoves are inexpensive and convenient for cooking. One butane canister will last about an hour on the high setting. However, butane is highly explosive and is hazardous to store. Fire authorities caution against storing butane in a home or garage. The butane cooker should be used outdoors to prevent carbon monoxide buildup and fire hazard.

Propane Cooking

Propane is convenient for cooking because of the availability of inexpensive 20 pound propane cylinders. However, a propane barbeque grill uses a lot of fuel. A small single burner propane cooking stove will use less propane. A 20 pound cylinder will power a small 10,000 BTU cooking stove for about 44 hours.

If you use propane for cooking and boiling water an hour a day, you will need nine 20 pound tanks a year. To conserve fuel, use some of the other cooking methods described in this chapter to supplement propane.

You may need a converter hose to connect the propane stove to a 20 pound propane cylinder. Check the manufacturer's instructions and precautions.

Fire authorities caution against storing extra propane in a home or garage. Propane cooking requires a lot of fuel storage. **If you don't have a safe place to store propane, select another option for cooking.**

Chapter Fifteen
Security

If you are prepared, the biggest concern may be to guard your provisions from those who did not prepare and from a possible government confiscation.

While the security recommendations sound extreme, the realities of a situation as severe as an EMP, suggest that one plan for self-defense.

Ideally, you can survive independently and safely on a large rural property partly wooded, near a water source. The large property will allow you to observe intruders before they get close to your home. The property will allow you to gather natural sources of food and collect from a continuous water source.

The ideal scenario is to live in your survival retreat before the EMP. This will allow you time to prepare the property and avoid the travel risk during the evacuations.

If you have the option, a brick house is better than wood sided because of the protection from high power rifles. It is also more difficult for intruders to burn it down.

If you are in an urban or suburban area and do not have a stocked retreat, your best option is to work together in a closed community. You can work with other neighbors to create and defend a secure border.

The community should assess the talent of the individuals and assign leadership roles to security responsibilities. Areas of assignment would be; firearm training, non-lethal weapon building and training, scouting teams, communications, immediate action deployment teams, surveillance, community checkpoints, patrols, and home defense modifications.

The U.S. Army Survival Guide will provide useful tips in group survival leadership.

What about retreating to an RV?

Recreational vehicles are not a good option as a retreat because of security risks. The walls are too thin for protection from bullets. They are obvious targets for refugee evacuees. A driven RV is more likely to run out of gas on the road to the retreat.

Parking an RV permanently inside of a stationary pole barn is a possible option. It is not visible by intruders and there is added protection from gunfire in the barn. Monitoring the perimeter while avoiding detection will be easier inside of the barn. However, it is important to maintain good ventilation to reduce the carbon monoxide emissions created by heating or cooking inside of a building.

How do you avoid detection?

During the survival stage, it is most important to be as invisible as possible to strangers to avoid confrontations. The lights at night should be blocked by "black out curtains" on the windows. Cooking smells and smoke should be minimized out doors. A location on top of a high hill is most conducive to being avoided by hungry and exhausted refugees and for visualizing intruders. This is the military "high-ground" advantage. To avoid detection by potential looters remember that noise and smells travel further in fog and snowy conditions and near woods or rock walls. A thermal inversion, an atmospheric condition, when the cooking smoke stays near the ground, is more likely at dusk and dawn.

"..when the failure of police and emergency services becomes protracted, the lawless element of society may emerge. For example, Hurricane Katrina in August 2005 damaged cell phone towers and radio antennas that were crucial to the operation of emergency communications. Protracted blackout of the power grid caused generators supporting emergency communications to exhaust their fuel supplies or fail from overuse. Consequently government, police and emergency services were severely impacted in their ability to communicate with the public and with each other. Looting, violence and other criminal activities were serious problems in the aftermath of Katrina." [91]

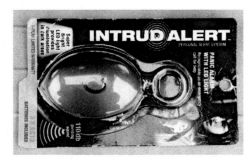

Use a panic alarm and trip wire to detect intruders

What if you are discovered by intruders?

[91] Dr. Foster, John S. Jr, et al, "*Critical National Infrastructures*", April 2008 p 151

In most situations, you will want to establish if the intruder is a friend or stranger. You should pre-arrange for friends who know your address to communicate by CB communication when they near your home. Binoculars should be available for confirmation at a distance. Your family should decide in advance if charity will be distributed and where it will be distributed. It is a good idea to do this anonymously perhaps through a local church. Evacuees could be directed to the church, a good distance from the survival community.

During the survival and isolation stage, methods to monitor intruders should be created. Large family groups could have guards on duty. A battery operated trip alarm could be devised by using a pocket personal alarm attached to a trip wire. The wire would surround the house.

The windows can be alarmed with solar powered alarms. A 12 volt motion detector powered by solar energy could be placed near the home. Loud alarms may frighten intruders. Bullhorns can be purchased and used to demand intention and to announce warnings. If the intruder proceeds toward the house and ignores the warnings, a warning shot may dissuade them.

Intruders could be fenced from the property using barbed wire or old fencing found in a local field. Two layers of fencing will slow the intruders down while you prepare. Barbed wire should not be too visible to the intruders. It could be coiled on the ground near the home. Remember to leave an opening for your own access.

Smoke grenades, stun guns, bow and arrows, chemical sprays and tazers are self-defense options available at gun stores. Primitive weapons like stones, bolas (rocks swirled from a rope and thrown), and slingshots can also be employed.

A .22 caliber rifle for small game and target practice is a reasonable investment. A deer rifle of the caliber used in the local area or a shotgun for birds could also be used for warning shots.

All family members should know how to load, maintain and shoot the guns. The .22 is best for practice because the ammunition is less expensive. All guns should be used occasionally. Hunting guns can serve a dual purpose of small game and self defense.

If you anticipate a gun fight, a steel wall or steel door is necessary to stop high caliber bullets. Perhaps a heavy wheelbarrow can be rolled from window to window. Steel plates at shooting positions can be strategically placed. The inside rooms are safer for the family. Plywood should be installed over windows when violence is anticipated. The plywood will not protect you from high velocity bullets, but it will hide your presence and movement within the structure.

Consider replacing your doors with steel doors. Add the best deadbolt lock you can. In addition, add a door security bar. This will make it much more difficult for someone to ram through your door.

For self defense practice, a .22 revolver is a good choice because the ammunition is the same as a .22 rifle. The ammunition is inexpensive and readily available. Every region may differ in the availability of certain guns and ammunition.

For protection you will want more stopping power than a .22 can provide. We chose a Czechoslovakian made, CZ75 with a four inch barrel as a good option for an inexpensive, but quality, handgun. Check to make sure the preloaded magazines are in good supply in your area. Each adult in the retreat should have one rifle and one hand gun for self defense.

.22 revolver, 9 mm automatic, and .22 rifle

Ammunition should be sufficient for target practice every month. Ammunition may not be available again for several years. Ammunition may be the currency for the survival duration. Extra ammunition should be purchased for bartering.

Several preloaded magazines should be stored for the semi automatic hand gun. Store extra magazines for use and for trade

The ammunition should be in air tight containers stored with silica gel packet desiccants.

Cleaning supplies for the guns should be purchased and available at the retreat home

The guns should be stored in a locked gun box with quick access keypad or thumbprint that is protected from EMP. Mace or pepper spray is a good alternative self defense weapon if you are in an urban area.

Local and state laws should be checked in advance. Some states allow lethal force to protect your family from an intruder, called a "castle doctrine" and some do not. Remember that you should not use more force, or fire more often, than necessary to defend you. It is predictable that when the government returns to normal and power is restored, prosecutions for self defense crimes will begin.

In our security preparation, we attended a firearm training class and were advised of the following basic self defense tactic. Do not confront an intruder in your home intentionally. If an intruder invades your home at night, call the police from a cell phone in your bedroom closet, announce to the intruder that you are armed and have called the police. If they do not respond or do not leave your home, and they approach your door, warn them again. You may consider firing through the hollow indoor door.

If a military approaches your community or retreat, you should hide your weapons, at least until you know which military is present. You may have to evaluate if it is the U.S. military, foreign military, United Nations, a State Guard, a militia or paramilitary group and measure your response as necessary. You should retain the guns for self protection, if you can. In a future chapter we will suggest options for the threat of government confiscation.

Chapter Sixteen
Medicine

If your pharmacy will allow you to order an advance supply of prescription medicine that you continue to use and replenish through a "first in first out" cycle, it is a good option. Order as much future supply as permitted, but monitor the expiration dates.

In addition to our normal prescription medicines, we purchased medications that are available over the counter and were prescribed in the past decades for common ailments. Silver, iodine, castor oil, and magnesia are medicines from the last century and are currently available as non-prescription items. Follow the label directions on all medicine.

What do you do when the prescribed medicines run out and there is no physician or pharmacy available?

When your emergency supplies are depleted and there is no further source of traditional medicine, there are alternative medicines in the form of holistic nutrition and herbal medicines. We anticipate being isolated from medical care due to security concerns, contamination concerns or lack of providers.

Some natural treatments are remarkably effective. There are excellent books on alternative therapies and herbal therapies. These would be essential for the survival library.

In all herbal treatments start with very small doses. The following are some of the alternative medicines commonly reported or in the U.S. Army guide that you might have available in your survival supplies:

1. Garlic tea for infections. Garlic does inhibit bacteria growth.

2. Cranberry juice for urinary tract infections. The tannin in cranberry juice prevents bacteria from adhering to the wall of the bladder.

3. Cloves (seasoning) for toothaches. Soak the dry seeds near the tooth to release the clove oil for 30 minutes.

4. Cayenne pepper or chili powder mixed with oil or lotion for external muscle pain rub. Capsaicin is a central ingredients in some pain rubs at doses of less than .075%. (less than 1%)

5. Cinnamon to help reduce blood sugar levels. Less than a half teaspoon a day has been used in studies.

6. Meat tenderizer containing papain or bromelain applied to the skin for bites and stings. These chemicals destroy the protein in the venom when applied to the injury. Use 1 part tenderizer to 4 parts water.

7. Mentholated eucalyptus chest rubs applied on the skin for foot fungus and muscle pain.

8. Iodine tincture for cuts and wounds. Iodine is an effective skin antiseptic. It was used effectively by some wounded civil war soldiers. A word of caution, some people are allergic to iodine.

9. Chicory root for constipation by making a tea with a small section of root. Chicory root can be applied externally to the skin for scratches, sunburn, bites and rashes. A caution, chicory can also cause allergic symptoms in those sensitive to the ragweed, daisy and marigold family of plants.

10. Bug repellent options are: thyme, parsley, basil and garlic.

11. For bee, wasp and scorpion stings, apply baking soda paste to the skin.

12. For diarrhea diseases, drink a weak tannic acid tea made from the bark of trees. A caution, too much tannic acid can hurt the kidneys. Bananas, rice, applesauce, tea and toast are foods currently recommended after diarrhea.

13. Tannic acid solution can be applied externally to burns, wounds, and poison ivy. Tannic acid solution can be made by boiling tree bark or walnuts in water, soaking sterile bandages in the solution for 10 minutes, and cooling before applying to the skin. Tannic acid is an astringent and will turn the water brown. Teas contain tannic acid.

14. Boil walnuts in water and apply the cooled water to the affected skin as an antifungal agent.

What about bites and stings?

99% of poisonous snake bites in the U.S. are the bites of pit vipers, including rattlesnakes, copperheads and water moccasins (also called cottonmouths). The two fang marks of pit vipers may be noticeable at the bite and intense pain within five minutes is characteristic.

In a quarter of poisonous snake bites, the snake does not inject poison.

The survival supply list includes a Sawyer ®Extractor kit that can effectively suck out the toxin. You should purchase the kit and study the instructions for use.

Most fatal bites are caused by insects and spiders, not snakes. Stingers of bees, wasps, hornets, yellow jackets and ants should be removed. Use baking soda to make a paste to apply to the sting.

Centipedes can cause severe pain, redness and swelling with their fanged bites. Millipedes cause burning and itching when their glands produce a toxin that touches our skin.

Many caterpillars have venom-containing hairs that can cause burning, redness, swelling and tissue death. [92] Apply and remove adhesive tape to extract the broken caterpillar hairs that remain on the skin.

Insect infestation can be prevented. The indoor spray repellants that are applied once a year may be a good choice for application to the basement wall/floor junction. The insecticide label is the law and should be well studied for your family's protection. Thorough cleaning and sanitizing and airing laundry and bedding in the sunlight will reduce the potential for insect infestation.

Boric acid powder can be mixed with water into a paste to control cockroaches, termites, ants, and fleas. If there is an infant in the home, use boric acid with caution because of toxic accumulation in their bodies.

---

[92] U.S. Army, U.S. Army Special Forces Medical Handbook, p 12-5

What about rat infestations?

Rats are adaptable and may survive well. If desperate, they may be an important part of the survival diet, if they have not been poisoned. Rats have been consumed as food in destitute environments. Rats common in urban areas have poor vision but a strong sense of smell. That will make them easy to trap. They will follow the same path as other rats in their colony from their burrow to the food source You can observe the greasy marks along walls they follow consistently. Their paths normally follow a wall. They also chew on rocks and wooden beams frequently to wear down their incisor teeth that continue to grow during their lives. You can look for teeth marks on those surfaces. They are territorial and will remain within their colony and defined boundary.

They are also aggressive in defending their territory and can be dangerous to humans. A rat bite should cause an immediate plan to exterminate them from your retreat area.

Rats should be handled carefully with tools because of the likelihood of fleas and diseases known to be transmitted by fleas of rats.

Chapter Seventeen
Survival Health Issues

This section will address some of the diseases and health concerns when living in a primitive environment. Also the basics of preventing infections through sanitary practices are described.

How do you prevent diseases?

A family that lives in an isolated area will escape contagions that are frequent in evacuation centers or refugee camps. If an acquaintance appears at your shelter and you choose to allow them to stay, it is a good idea to require an isolation period in a nearby shelter or tent, especially if there is an active epidemic.

Diseases of the 19th century such as, tetanus, dysentery, typhus, tuberculosis, nutritional deficiencies and cholera may reappear. The best option for the survivalist is to keep your family isolated from the general community to avoid the airborne and common vector diseases.

Cholera or dysentery organisms may be found in surface water and will cause extreme diarrhea, fever, and vomiting. The dehydration caused by cholera or any major diarrhea episode can be treated with oral rehydration therapy. Oral rehydration salts are available in packages of three for mixing with water and cost about $9 from sources on the internet or in camping supply stores.

They are also available in liquid form and sold with infant medications.

The victims of cholera may recover in one to two weeks but will continue to discharge the organism in their stools.

Diarrhea illnesses can also be spread through the feces of birds and animals and the indirect transmission of the organisms on flies and crawling insects. Although your retreat can be free of disease, flying insects can transmit the disease from miles away.

Isolation of the toilet facility of infected family members and the sealing and burying of wastes will prevent the spread of illness.

What other diseases are of concern?

Typhus--- is transmitted by bites from lice, fleas or mites. It causes high fever, rash, headache and pain. It may be fatal. Your retreat or home can be treated with insecticide and careful cleaning to avoid infestations.

Sufficient supplies of insecticide and regular cleaning or daily airing of laundry in the sun, if washing is not possible, will help prevent infestations that lead to this disease.

Tetanus—there could be frequent exposure to tetanus, a clostridium bacteria naturally found in the soil. It is the same family of bacteria that also causes botulism, a poison in improperly canned foods. Tetanus bacteria produce a toxin that causes extreme muscle spasms for weeks. It earned the nickname "lockjaw" because of the muscle contractions in the mouth and throat. Presuming that medical attention to diagnose and treat will not be available, we should all receive a booster vaccination now at our physician's office. The vaccination should provide protection for about five to ten years.

Typhoid Fever- a disease transmitted by infected sewage and poor sanitary practices. A percentage of those infected will remain chronic carriers. "Typhoid Mary" was an example. It is caused by a form of streptococcus bacteria that could be treated with antibiotics, if antibiotics were available.

Rabies--- may be a concern because evacuees will be living closer to wild animal habitats in the wild. Skunks and bats are particularly of concern. The herd immunity provided by annual pet vaccinations will be reduced because of the lack of veterinary care for a long period and wild packs of dogs. The risk may be reduced by the elimination of most animals for survivor food during the first few months.

Nutritional diseases--- these diseases caused by a lack of certain vitamins were common in the last century. A multi-vitamin is necessary in the survival supplies. The following information and symptoms may be helpful in identifying a vitamin deficiency disease.

Pellagra is a Vitamin B deficiency disease. It causes loss of strength and loss of weight and a sore, red tongue.

Beri beri is a B1 (thiamin) deficiency disease. It causes weakness and muscle atrophy.

Goiter may be caused by an iodine deficiency. It causes swelling of the thyroid at the base of the throat.

Rickets is a calcium deficiency. It causes aching of bones.

Scurvy is a Vitamin C deficiency disease. It causes swollen and bleeding gums and loosening of teeth.

Night blindness may result from a Vitamin A deficiency.

Some of these deficiencies could be treated with wild foods described in the preceding Food chapter.

What conditions could result from extreme heat and cold?

We will be working harder outdoors in the heat and cold extremes than we have in the past. Indoors, the lack of fuel will limit our ability to affect the temperature. This will make us more prone to heat and cold affects.

A U.S. Army Medical Handbook describes four factors for heat stress; air temperature, relative humidity, air movement and heat radiation. As the temperature rises, physical activity should be reduced.

At 50% humidity a 95F degree day feels like 107. At 70% humidity the same 95 degree day feels like 124.

Heat injuries

Heat cramps- are caused by excessive salt loss through sweating. A .1% salt water cool drink in the shade will help.

Heat exhaustion- is caused by reduced peripheral circulation due to salt loss and dehydration. It is treated in the same manner as heat cramps.

The cool drink of the .1% salt water dilution will provide some treatment. We previously described in detail how to make the two step dilution in the Food chapter.

First, mix ½ teaspoon of salt into 8 ounces of water,

Next, take only ½ teaspoon of the salt dilution above

and mix it with another 8 ounce glass of plain water.

The victim should avoid re-exposure to heat until fully treated.

Heatstroke- is caused by a breakdown of the body heat regulating mechanism. The onset is sudden with collapse and loss of consciousness. Convulsions may occur. Death may come rapidly. The victim's temperature must be reduced rapidly. Remove their clothes and place them in cold water or wet them down and fan them. When the temperature drops to 102 degrees, dry the patient and wrap in blankets. Continue to monitor their temperature every ten minutes for the next two days. You may have to continue heating and cooling their body during that time. Consult the U.S. Army Medical handbook or another comprehensive emergency medical book for treatment options.

Dehydration

After the feeling of thirst and loss of appetite and sleepiness caused by dehydration the victim's body temperature will further increase and they will become nauseated. When 15% of the body is dehydrated and temperatures are above 90 degrees, dehydration is probably fatal.[93] When the temperature is high, activity must be reduced.

Cold Injuries

Cold injuries are affected by weather, temperature, humidity, precipitation and wind. Clothes should be worn loose and in layers. The inner layers should be removed during exertion. If they become wet with

---

[93] Department of the Army Field Manual, <u>Survival</u> FM 21-76 October 1970 p231

perspiration, they lose their insulating quality and wet clothing will feel cold. Starvation, injuries and fatigue will increase the risk of cold injuries.

The following chart reveals the affect of wind speed (rows) on temperature (columns). The temperature in the boxes indicates the cold stress that the individual will endure at that wind and temperature.

Affect of wind speed on temperature

	20F	15F	10F	5F	0	-5	-10
5	13	7	1	-5	-11	-16	-22
10	9	3	-4	-10	-16	-22	-28
15	6	0	-7	-13	-19	-26	-32
20	4	-2	-9	-15	-22	-29	-35
25	3	-4	-11	-17	-24	-31	-37
30	1	-5	-12	-19	-26	-33	-39
35	0	-7	-14	-21	-27	-34	-41
40	-1	-8	-15	-22	-29	-36	-43
45	-2	-9	-16	-23	-30	-37	-44
50	-3	-10	-17	-24	-31	-38	-45
55	-3	-11	-18	-25	-32	-39	-46

94

Cold injuries are classified as first to fourth degrees. Frostbite is not a classification, but only describes how the injury occurred.

Cold Injury Degree

First degree cold injuries- display red, hot dry skin after re-warming. Intense itching and burning may be present. Swelling starts in hours and can last ten days unless

---

[94] National Weather Service, New Wind Chill Chart,(data) www.crh.noaa.gov/ddc

physical activity is reduced. Peeling of injured skin will begin in 5-10 days and last a month.

Second degree cold injuries- display the signs of first degree injury plus blisters. The blisters become black and eventually separate from easily traumatized skin.

Third degree cold injuries- cause death of the skin. Swelling occurs in six days. The victim will not feel the injury until after two weeks. Then they will have pain for months. The injury becomes black and hard and finally separates after two months.

Fourth degree cold injuries- cause tissue death of the body part affected including the bone. The tissue will progress to gangrene and mummification.

Cold injuries are progressive. The longer the exposure, the deeper the injury. The first sign of cold injury is the loss of sensation of cold and a pleasant feeling of warmth. To treat, warm the affected body part by holding it to another warm body part and protect from further injury. Immediate shelter from the cold is important.

The severity of heat and cold injuries and the long term implications reveal a need to study preventive treatment thoroughly. Temperature and weather conditions will play a larger role in our lifestyle during the power grid emergency.

We suggest you purchase the U.S. Army Medical Handbook or similar Guide to study and keep it in the survival retreat as a reference. Options for heat and cold treatment are included in the text.

How do you sanitize surfaces?

We have previously described purifying water. The remainder of this chapter will discuss disinfecting surfaces, shelter sanitation, personal hygiene and installing pit privies, and pail toilets.

When running water is not available and sewer systems are not functioning, the filthy conditions will lead to serious intestinal diseases. It is possible to avoid the filthy conditions, even without running water and sewage, with extreme precautions in disinfection and disposal of wastes.

The food preparation and living quarters should be disinfected often to avoid skin and intestinal infections. This will also result in fewer insect infestations. The more people using the locations, the more frequently it needs to be sanitized.

To sanitize any hard surface, mix a 50-100 ppm chlorine solution for wetting a cleaning cloth. The concentration should not exceed 200 ppm. The following is one formula;

1. Mix 1 teaspoons of bleach (5% chlorine solution) into a gallon of water to create 65 ppm of chlorine for disinfection of surfaces. You can use your chlorine test kit to measure your concentration. Add additional bleach if the concentration goes below 50 ppm.

2. Note: If you are storing pool shock instead of bleach, you must reduce the 70% chlorine concentration to 5% first, by adding 1 ounce of pool shock to 14 ounces of water. The formula was provided in the Water chapter.

3. Before sanitizing, clean the surface with soap and rinse.

4. You can wet a cloth in this bleach solution or put the solution in a plastic spray bottle and spray and wipe with a cloth. The chlorine solution should remain on the surface for one minute to disinfect.

5. Let the solution air dry on the surface cleaned.

How do you sanitize eating utensils?

For disease protection, eating utensils, plates and drinking cups should not be shared until they are washed, rinsed and disinfected. This is the formula for sanitizing the food storage jars also.

The eating utensils and cups are disinfected using 50-100 ppm bleach and water solution after washing and rinsing.

1. You can mix 1 teaspoon (of the 5% bleach into a gallon of water. (65 ppm) If you are using the powdered pool shock, remember to dilute it first to a 5% solution with water.

2. Wash and rinse the eating utensils, plates and cups.

3. Sanitize the clean utensils, plates and cups by soaking them in the 50-100 ppm bleach solution for one minute and then air dry. Do not exceed 200 ppm. This is the standard used for restaurant eating utensils.

What are the risks to using chlorine?

The prior chapter on disinfecting water should be reviewed for risks associated with using and storing chlorine. Chlorine should never be mixed with acid or other cleaners and is toxic to the lungs and will irritate any mucus membranes. Chlorine is heavier than air and vapors from a spill will concentrate near the floor.

You should have a plentiful supply of plastic gloves because the sanitizing bleach solution can be hard on your hands and absorbed through the skin.

Use hydrogen peroxide, iodine or alcohol instead of chlorine to disinfect skin infections.

How will your family treat toilet waste?

When the water stops running and the toilets do not flush, the toilet should be relocated outdoors (if weather permits) or indoors on a plastic lined 5 gallon paint bucket with a lid. To prevent odor and flies from transmitting disease, you should store cat litter or sand in a bucket near the toilet for pouring immediately on excrement.

The sealed garbage bag containing daily waste should be buried daily outdoors as deeply as possible, but above the perched water table and 100 feet from your closest water source.

How do you dig your own outdoor toilet?

It is better that the toilet be outside during reasonable weather than indoors. The outdoor toilet location should consider the slope and the water run off after a rain to protect the water supply source. Construction techniques for an outdoor latrine have been forgotten for a century.

The following is practical information from a U.S. Army Medical Handbook;

In temporary camp, deep pit latrines are constructed. Deep pit latrines are not used in rocky or frozen soil or where the water table is high. Trenches are two foot wide, seven feet long and up to six feet deep. Tents can be placed over the latrines for privacy and ropes should be placed to guide users from the home to the latrine at night. A wooden box without a bottom, and a hole on top, with the hinged toilet seat affixed, can be placed over the trench. The wooden box with the toilet lid can be relocated to another trench as needed.

A burn out latrine is used in rocky or frozen soil or when the water table is high. It is for feces only. Construct with a metal 55 gallon drum, buried halfway and covered with a fly proof wooden seat. Burn out daily or when half full, until only ash remains and then bury the ash. [95]

How will you bathe?

Another useful item in the survival supplies is a simple solar camping shower. These are inexpensive and will provide soothing comfort when you can take a shower with warm water.

A solar pool heater can provide hot water for bathing. A solar blanket pool cover can be placed on a child's plastic pool to heat water a few inches deep outdoors on sunny days for a warm bath. You can also use black plastic in place of the solar pool heater blanket to warm the water.

---

[95] U. S. Army, Institute for Military Assistance, <u>U.S. Army Special Forces Medical Handbook</u>, ST 31-91B, March 1982 p 20-9

Another option for hot water is to buy a solar pool heating panel, available at an internet site for $226. These are designed for a pump, but possibly modified to use gravity or a manual operated pump.

How do you care for clothes?

Needles, threads and buttons should be purchased for the expected repairs required after bleaching and hard washing and sun drying. This is a good time to store all of your old garments instead of throwing them out.

Clothes can be washed with every heavy rain during a water shortage.

Handkerchiefs are important for containing respiratory infections and should be washed, soaked in a disinfecting solution of chlorine, rinsed and allowed to dry in the sun before reusing.

Bedding, clothing and towels should also be washed, rinsed, bleached and exposed to sunlight as often as possible. If the water supply is limited, spray the chlorine solution and expose the bedding to sunlight for six hours if possible. This will prevent insect infestations and diseases they carry.

Clothespins, a clothesline, and detergent are on the supply list. Used wash water should be buried in a hole in the ground, not thrown in surface water. It is sewage. Movement through the soil will decontaminate it.

Clothes should be changed daily and washed, or at least exposed to sunlight each day, to avoid infections and insect infestations, especially socks and underwear.

If your shoes are wet, stuff them with dry grass, newspapers or moss overnight to help dry them out.

What personal hygiene habits are important?

Shaving will eventually be dispensed with, when the razors are dull. No need to increase the risk of skin irritation with dull blades. One civil war hero died of tetanus from a dull razor nick. Short trimmed finger and toe nails will also reduce infections.

Wipe hands with disposable baby wipes after using the toilet and before food or drink preparation. Thousands of baby wipes should be in your survival supplies.

Face and eyelids can be washed with baby shampoo and rinsed with disinfected water to remove allergens and avoid infections.

Any red or swollen skin or insect bites should be considered infected. Alcohol, iodine or hydrogen peroxide should be applied to these infections daily and after any dirty exposure.

If you run out of dental supplies, baking soda, soap or salt can be used for toothpaste. A small green twig can be used for a toothbrush. Grind one end of the twig with your teeth to create bristles.

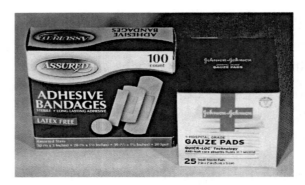

Stock up on bandages

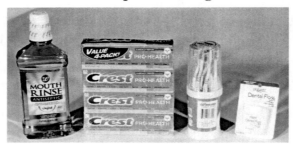

and dental supplies.

Chapter Eighteen
Fire Safety and Burn Prevention

Fire will be a constant concern. There will be open fires for cooking and heating. Looters could start fires to drive out inhabitants or simply for warmth. The fires may start unintentionally or by arson, but either way they will go out of control due to lack of water, working hydrants or fuel for fire equipment.

How do you fireproof your supplies?

The retreat home could have a fireproof room to secure the essentials. This room could be hidden as part of its construction. Concrete block walls could be added to a corner of an existing concrete foundation.

Earthen or stone cellars can be built into existing hillsides or basements. The family could seek shelter elsewhere during the fire and return to their stored and protected provisions after the fire.

Fire extinguishers are an essential item. Use of open flame for light, heat, and cooking greatly increases the chance of accidental fire. You should have several fire extinguishers conveniently located throughout the house.

What types of Fire Extinguishers do you need?

Fire Extinguishers may be labeled as:

> A- for wood/paper
>
> B- for liquids like grease or gasoline
>
> C- for electrical
>
> D- flammable metals

Some fire extinguishers are classified in multiple classes. The label may show the above letter or show pictures of the materials above.

Fire extinguishers may contain: Halon, or Water- (contains water and compressed gas for Type A fires only), or Carbon Dioxide- for Class B and C fires. Carbon dioxide extinguishers may need longer (about 20 minutes) of application because of re-flash potential.

What are useful fire safety recommendations?

Large quantities of baking soda should be available as a fire extinguisher. Baking soda extinguishes fire by releasing carbon dioxide when heated. The carbon dioxide is heavier than air and it smothers the flames.

A heavy blanket may smother a fire and should be kept handy.

Water conducts electricity and can cause electrical shock. Never apply water to an electrical fire.

Oil fires are the most dangerous. If water is applied, the water will go to the bottom and boil, spraying hot oil. Smothering an oil fire is best.

Fire extinguishers should be pointed at the base of the fire.

What about rescuing victims of fire?

The U.S. Army Medical Handbook recommends that if the victim's clothes are on fire, put the victim on the floor and smother the flames with a coat, rug or blanket. If there is boiling water scalding the victim, rip off the clothes to reduce exposure to the hot fluid. To rescue a patient in a burning room, tie a wet cloth around your face and hold your breath and stay low.

Burn Injury Degree

The following is a brief summary of the U.S. Army calculation of depth (degree) of burn;

First degree; only the outer layer of epidermis is burned. Reddened, tingling, and painful skin. Skin peels and recovers within seven days.

Second degree; most of the thickness of the skin is burned, very painful.. Blisters, weeping surface, and mild edema (swelling) is present. Skin heals in two to three weeks.

Third degree; the full thickness of skin is destroyed. Edema is significant. A scab will form and peel in three weeks. Scar tissue will cover the burn.[96]

You should cool the burn immediately with water, ice or snow to stop the burning process. The wound must be kept sterile.

---

[96] U S Army U S. Army Special Forces Medical Handbook, ST31-91B, p 10-1

Chapter Nineteen
Response to Government Dictates

What are the government plans?

The federal government already has plans and agencies for large national emergencies. During the past decade the homeland defense forces and civil authority defense forces have undergone significant reorganizations.

The government will deploy the military in a U.S. Northern Command, a unified command combining existing homeland defenses and civil support missions.

The U.S. Northern Command will be directed by the President or Secretary of Defense. It will provide defense support of civil authorities and include consequence management operations.

CBRNE (Chemical, biological, radiological, nuclear and high yield explosive incident in the homeland) Consequence Management Forces were first deployed in 2008.

The degree of intended military operation in a disaster is demonstrated by the Catastrophic Disaster Response Incident Command. The forces include Health and Medical, Shelter and Mass Care under the Emergency Services Division. The Law Enforcement Division includes Perimeter Control and Investigations. The Logistics Section controls Communication, Medical and Food.

They boast an Initial Response Resource team that can shelter and feed 30,000 victims in 72 hours.

In an EMP, that will not be nearly enough. The 2010 health care reform bill included a medical force that can be called involuntarily for a national emergency.

Will the government confiscate food?

"Social order likely would decay if a food shortage were protracted. A government that cannot supply the population with enough food to preserve health and life could face anarchy."[97]

During the power outage, it is possible that the government will confiscate survival supplies and food for redistribution. The authorities may not care that you prepared for the outage long before the supplies were depleted.

"Hoarding deprives government of the opportunity to ration local food supplies to ensure that all people are adequately fed in the event of a food shortage."[98]

U.S. Representative Roscoe Bartlett encouraged preparation in a Congressional hearing, "..if you are preparing for something like this in advance, say, years ahead, you are now a patriot, you are stimulating the economy but if you do it hours before it happens, now you are a hoarder and timing is very critical"[99]

---

[97] Dr. Foster, John S. Jr, et al, "Critical National Infrastructures", April 2008 p 134

[98] Dr. Foster, John S. Jr, et al, "Critical National Infrastructures", April 2008 p 134

[99] Rep, Bartlett, Roscoe, Threat Posed by Electromagnetic Pulse (EMP) Attack, Committee on Armed Services, July 10, 2008, p. 29

Will the existing government have control?

The ad hoc or pseudo governments, foreign governments, militias, clans, gangs, or cooperatives could challenge the U.S. government for control of regions.

You will be aware of the government actions based on the police scanners and radio transmissions. If you find that there is a question of authority, you should maintain secrecy about your preparations.

You may ultimately be forced to give up your supplies. The EMP Commission addressed the government's concern about individuals with plentiful supplies and the threat of anarchy to the government.

What about refugee camps?

As a possible outcome, you may also be forced to join the refugee camps. It is a better idea to avoid this option as long as possible to avoid the communicable diseases. This risk should be balanced against the security risk of active gangs. The goal should be to avoid the refugee camps until later in the outage, if a steady stream of organized supplies and shelters has been established and order is restored. If you are alerted to chaos in the temporary shelters, it is best to survive on your own.

Chapter Twenty
Bartering

If the financial system has collapsed and money is not available, barter may be the only way to acquire essential items that you may need. It is also a way to build a community survival network of friends.

Until the grid failure is over, you will be more likely to obtain needed items by trading other needed goods than with money. Some people are collecting pre-1965 dimes for the silver content. Some people are collecting real gold pieces for this event. Paper dollars will be useful only during the first few weeks until the catastrophe is over.

"The financial infrastructure is highly dependent on electronic systems...Virtually all transactions involving banks and other financial institutions happen electronically. Virtually all record keeping of financial transactions are stored electronically... The electronic technologies that are the foundation of the financial infrastructure are potentially vulnerable to EMP." [100]

In our opinion, the most valuable bartering items will be the useful and basic survival needs, bandages, ammunition, disinfectant, tools, etc.

When the power failure ends, we anticipate reclaiming our paper investments from financial institutions. The data will be stored in some manner that can be retrieved if the institutions and government survive.

[100] Dr. Foster, John S. Jr, et al, *"Critical National Infrastructures"*, April 2008 p 88

What supplies are good for barter?

Anything that is useful and that is in short supply will be valuable for bartering. It is best to select items with a long shelf life. Anything that you have in excess may be useful for barter. Here is a list of items you may want to buy in excess for barter or charity:

Aluminum foil

Ammunition

Bandages and gauze pads

Bleach (you can make this from Pool Shock powder)

Books on survival

Candles

Canned food

Charged batteries (could be a service you provide)

Dental supplies

Duct Tape

Flashlights

Battery operated or hand tools (saw, drill, etc.)

Matches

Medicine

Nails

Soap

Solar battery chargers

Solar Oven (make them for trade)

Toothbrushes

Chapter Twenty-One
Survival Supplies

The following is a shopping list for survival supplies. The hardware and pharmacy supplies should be purchased in large quantities.

If you do not need them, you can use them for bartering for other items. You can choose to use them for charity, too.

Electronics Store

CB radio, portable DC powered

Police scanner, portable DC powered

AM/FM/shortwave radio, portable DC powered

Crank powered emergency radio

VHF police, marine and weather scanner, portable DC powered

Amateur radio transmitter and receiver, portable and DC powered (study book for testing and license)

12 VDC marine band radios

12 V deep cycle batteries

Rechargeable batteries of all sizes needed for battery operated equipment

Battery Conditioner

Solar battery chargers

Battery Tender®

Hardware Store Supplies

Fire extinguishers

Duct tape

Batteries, (rechargeable, low self discharge, nickel metal hydride)

Barbed wire

Clothesline, clothespins

Wire, nails, nuts, bolts, twine,

Screwdrivers, wrenches, hammer, 2 sets of basic tools

Waterproof matches

Wooden box matches stored in metal container with silica desiccant

Water filters and water filter pitcher

Glass jars or stainless steel containers

Fishing line

Mouse traps

Wasp spray

Thermometers

Aluminum foil- for cooking and equipment

Clear wrap

Hardware cloth or screening

Metal garbage cans with lids for storage of food and supplies

Plastic 5 gallon empty paint buckets with lids labeled for storing and carrying water with lids

Plastic 5 gallon buckets with lids labeled for storing and disposing of waste (make-shift toilet)

Contractor bags or strong garbage bags for lining toilet waste containers

Shovels for digging water or pit privy

Personal "trip" alarms

Charcoal

Saws

Knives

Siphons for water and gas

String or twine

Rope

Bungee cords

Cat litter

Boric acid powder

Branch cutter

Propane line converter

35 gallon water tank

Faucet for water tank

Plumbers tape

Solar cooker or materials to build solar cooker

Insecticides- for ants, mites, roaches, flies, centipedes

Children's plastic pool

Pool solar blanket

Wood, for temporary construction

Disposable plastic gloves

Wheelbarrow

Metal boxes for storage

Plastic bins or metal cans for dry storage

Pool Shock powder containing chlorine only

Chorine test strips 0-200ppm

Camping store

Propane cook stove

Propane cylinders to store outside with grill

Propane grill

Cast iron kettle

Camp skillet

Campfire tripod

Propane catalytic heater

Tent wood burning stove

Insecticide

Mylar space blanket

Sawyer® Extractor

Flint striker firestarter

Internet Source

Desiccant silica gel packets

LDS or similar, bulk long term storage food in #10 cans; wheat, oats, pinto beans

Solar ovens, Global Sun Oven®

Swimming pool chlorine test kits

Solar dehydrators to dry vegetables and fruits

Faraday cage supplies and bags

Solar pool heaters

Water filters

Hand grinder for corn, wheat, oat milling

Drug store items

Wet wipes, (at least 1000 in quantity)

Toothpaste

Loperamide, anti-diarrhea medicine

White surgical tape

Aloe vera gel

Antihistamine, anti-allergy treatment

Alcohol thermometer, (replaced former mercury thermometers)

Diphenhydramine, antihistamine, allergy medicine

Providone-iodine 10%, antibacterial topical solution

Splinter forceps (tweezers)

Needle nose pliers

Wire cutter

Steel sewing needles

Extractor snake bite suction device (Sawyer® extractor), also for bee, wasp, scorpion stings

Respiratory Masks

Aspirin

Eye droppers

Ibuprofen

Triple antibiotic ointment

Heartburn relief medicine

Mucus relief, expectorant,

Bandages of all sizes and types including butterfly closures

Gauze pads

Calamine lotion

Campho-phenique®, antiseptic and parasiticide anti itch topical ointment.

Permethrin 1% cream, for mites and lice. Note: 1% is available over the counter, 5% requires a prescription.

Anti fungal ointment

Lidocaine- containing topical liquid for pain, itching and burns.

Silver hydrosol

Analgesic gel

Hand soap

Boric acid powder

Q-tips

Elastic bandage

Omega 3 fish oil gel caps

Prescription medications filled in advance

Baby shampoo

Cotton rounds

Deodorant

Vaseline

Mentholated chest rub

Multi vitamins

Oral Hydration Salts powdered electrolyte beverage mix, in case of dehydration

Feminine napkins, also for use as bandages

Fabric store

Cheesecloth

Black out cloth

Needle, heavy thread

Buttons

Patches

Scissors

Used Treadle sewing machine

Cotton cloth (used for making handkerchiefs and bandages)

Grocery items

Measuring Cups and spoons

Instant Coffee

Coffee filters

Olive Oil –96 pounds/per person

Vegetable seeds

Canned vegetables and fruits

Salt 10 pounds/per person

Rice 30 pounds/per person

Wheat 220 pounds/per person

Corn 50 pounds/ per person

Oats 20 pounds/ per person

Powdered milk 20 pounds/per person

Canned meats and fish, tuna, mackerel, salmon

Peanut butter

Canned nuts

Aluminum foil – for storage and cooking

Baking soda- for many purposes

Vinegar

Sugar

Dish cleaning soap

Laundry detergent

Baby shampoo

Bleach

Seasonings and spices

Ziploc bags gallon and sandwich size

Meat tenderizer containing papain or bromelain

Book store items

(see recommended reading list for book details)

Edible Plants

Weed identification book

Tree identification

Alternative remedies

Herbal remedies

Family Emergency Handbook or basic first aid guide

Amateur Radio training guide

Scout handbook for cooking methods, trapping

Maps, Local, county traffic maps with secondary roads

Holy Bibles

Alternative Energy

Batteries

Wilderness Survival

Medical handbook

Food Preservation Methods

See recommendations in the Recommended reading list

Gun store items

.22 gauge rifle

.22 handgun

9 mm handgun

Gun cleaning supplies

Lots of ammunition and magazines

Pepper spray

Taser gun

Bow and arrows

Binoculars/telescope

Compass

Magnesium/steel fire starter

Chapter Twenty-Two
Religion

Blessed is the one who reads aloud the words of the prophecy, and blessed are those who hear and who keep what is written in it; for the time is near.

Revelation 1:3

(New Revised Standard Version)

Faith

Now is the time to read the Bible and to seek a church where the Bible is understood as the word of God and the congregation is encouraged to bring their bibles. The study in faith will be critical knowledge in the midst of the survival period. Those who already know God will provide spiritual sustenance to others. They will improve the survival odds and the condition of others by sharing the wisdom of the scriptures.

You should have several Bibles in your survival library so that you can share with others. There will be many opportunities to speak publicly about your faith and an audience in need of the support. Infant dedications, baptisms and funerals will need scriptural support. As an example, the following scriptures would provide support for those feeling hopeless.

I believe that I shall see the goodness of the Lord in the land of the living.

Wait for the Lord;

be strong, and let your heart take courage;

wait for the Lord!

Psalm 27:13-14 (NRSV)

The Lord is a stronghold for the oppressed,

A stronghold in times of trouble.

And those who know your name put their trust in you,

for you, O Lord, have not forsaken those who seek you.

Psalm 9: 9-10 (NRSV)

Are any among you suffering? They should pray. Are any cheerful? They should sing songs of praise. Are any among you sick? They should call for the elders of the church and have them pray over them, anointing them with oil in the name of the Lord. The prayer of faith will save the sick, and the Lord will raise them up, and anyone who has committed sins will be forgiven. Therefore confess your sins to one another, and pray for one another, so that you may be healed. The prayer of the righteous is powerful and effective.

James 5: 13-16 (NRSV)

The following is Psalm 23, commonly read to bring support for those in illness or danger.

The Lord is my shepherd, I shall not want.

He makes me lie down in green pastures;

He leads me beside still waters;

he restores my soul.

He leads me in right paths

for his name's sake.

Even though I walk through the darkest valley,

I fear no evil;

For you are with me;

Your rod and your staff-

they comfort me.

You prepare a table before me

In the presence of my enemies;

You anoint my head with oil;

my cup overflows.

Surely goodness and mercy shall follow me

all the days of my life,

And I shall dwell in the house of the Lord

my whole life long.

Psalm 23 (NRSV)

The Lord's prayer is the prayer that Jesus taught the disciples. Many Christians repeat it often in extreme circumstances.

The Lord's Prayer

Our father, who art in heaven,

Hallowed be thy name.

Thy kingdom come,

Thy will be done,

on earth as it is in heaven.

Give us this day our daily bread;

And forgive us our trespasses, as we forgive those who trespass against us.

And lead us not into temptation,

but deliver us from evil.

For thine is the kingdom,

The power and the glory,

for ever and ever,

Amen

Matthew 6: 9-13 (King James Version)

Daily Bible Readings

A daily prayer and bible study will help to bring the community together and increase the motivation to endure difficulties.

Historical perspective

The EMP survivors should understand that mankind has witnessed extreme deprivation many times in history. The scriptures have offered wisdom and guidance for centuries in the text form. For thousands of years on stone and scrolls the same scriptures were quoted.

The fear of the Lord is the beginning of wisdom, and the knowledge of the Holy One is insight.

Proverbs 9:10 (NRSV)

As for mortals, their days are like grass;

They flourish like a flower of the field,

For the wind passes over it, and it is gone,

And its place knows it no more.

But the steadfast love of the Lord is from everlasting to everlasting on those who fear him,

And his righteousness to children's children,

To those who keep his covenant

And remember to do his commandments.

Psalm 103: 15-18 (NRSV)

Emotional reactions

There will be emotional reactions to the survival process. Impatience, anger, loneliness, fear, boredom and depression may be expressed. Bible study will be important to the physical and spiritual health of the family and community.

You must understand this, my beloved; let everyone be quick to listen, slow to speak, slow to anger, for your anger does not produce God's righteousness. Therefore rid yourselves of all sordidness and rank growth of wickedness, and welcome with meekness, the implanted word that has the power to save your souls.

James 1:19-21 (NRSV)

for God did not give us a spirit of cowardice, but rather a spirit of power and of love and of self discipline.

2 Timothy 1:7 (NRSV)

Group Support

Survival training has revealed that groups working together with leaders that fulfill their responsibilities have the best chance of survival. The leader should be responsible for each person's welfare and prevent arguments and strife. A feeling of mutual dependence is necessary to support each other. This attitude creates high morale and unity and enhances survival. These are lessons learned by the Army but also lessons provided by scripture.

Give instruction to the wise and they will become wiser still; teach the righteous and they will gain in learning.

Proverbs 9:9 (NRSV)

Owe no one anything, except to love one another; for the one who loves another has fulfilled the law. The commandments, "You shall not commit adultery; You shall not murder; You shall not steal; You shall not covet"; and any other commandment, are summed up in this word, "Love your neighbor as yourself". Love does no wrong to a neighbor; therefore, love is the fulfilling of the law.

Romans 13:8-10 (NRSV)

Charity

Questions of charity may cause anxiety. If you are in a defined community of known neighbors, you should plan strategies together. The survival environment will demand hard work. The practicalities of charity during survival will not be the same as charity in the present. Excess inventories will probably not be available to support those who are not contributing. Perhaps short term labor could be traded for food and necessities. Bible scriptures in Old Testament Proverbs address the practicality of the Judeo-Christian work ethic but also the blessings of the generous.

A slack hand causes poverty, but the hand of the diligent makes rich. A child who gathers in summer is prudent, but a child who sleeps in harvest brings shame.

Proverbs 10: 4-5 (NRSV)

Those who are generous are blessed, for they share their bread with the poor.

Proverbs 22: 9 (NRSV)

Go to the ant, you lazybones; consider its ways, and be wise. Without having any chief or officer or ruler, it prepares its food in summer, and gathers its sustenance in harvest. How long will you lie there, O lazybones? When will you rise from your sleep?

A little sleep, a little slumber,

A little folding of the hands to rest,

And poverty will come upon you like a robber, and want, like an armed warrior.

Proverbs 6: 6-11 (NRSV)

Crime

The lack of religious teaching and the decay of moral behavior in our culture has led to crimes in normal circumstances. In a survival situation crime will be more pronounced in the same population. The answer to civil obedience is taught in bible scripture.

How much better to get wisdom than gold?

To get understanding is to be chosen rather than silver.

The highway of the upright avoids evil;

those who guard their way preserve their lives.

Pride goes before destruction,

and a haughty spirit before a fall.

It is better to be of a lowly spirit among the poor

than to divide the spoil with the proud.

Proverbs 16: 16-19 (NRSV)

Besides this, you know what time it is, how it is now the moment for you to wake from sleep. For salvation is nearer to us now than when we became believers; the night is far gone, the day is near. Let us then lay aside the works of darkness and put on the armor of light; let us live honorably as in the day, not in reveling and drunkenness, not in debauchery and licentiousness, not in quarreling and jealousy. Instead, put on the Lord Jesus Christ, and make no provision for the flesh, to gratify its desires.

Romans 13:11-14 (NRSV)

Chapter Twenty-Three
The Aftermath

The EMP Commission concluded that a significant percentage of the U.S. population will perish from a massive solar storm or EMP attack that causes widespread and long term loss of power.

The foreign militaries that describe using an EMP against the U.S. refer to it as the "first strike". Based on these statements, the remnant of the U.S. population that survives may be under assault by a foreign military or U.N. control.

Survivors of a widespread outage will live in sparsely populated communities for a long time. It is unlikely that our nation will ever return to the economic prosperity and leisure that we now enjoy. However, family centered, religious and independent living may be a new standard. These will not be pleasant times though. The surviving population will suffer from the shock of deep personal losses. A military government will impose restrictions on freedom.

The Opportunity

"The de facto national policy of nakedness to all of our potentially EMP-armed enemies takes on ever more the character of national scale masochism. It is perverse, irrational, and assuredly not necessary or foreordained". [101] As Dr. Lowell Wood has stated, an EMP event is not certain. There is an opportunity to prevent catastrophic damage, although it is not the direction that our policy makers are moving toward.

The U.S. House passed a GRID Act in 2010 to protect the power grid. Unfortunately the U.S. Senate Energy Committee erased the protections in their version.

Congresswoman Yvette D. Clarke, chair of the Subcommittee on Emerging Threats, Cyber security, and Science and Technology, said in 2009, "Cyber and physical attacks against the grid could both be catastrophic and incredibly destructive events, but they are not inevitable. Protections can and must be put in place ahead of time to mitigate the impact of these attacks."[102]

We hope that the public will encourage their representatives to demand the power grid be protected. We also hope that our government is carefully monitoring potential missile launches and using missile defenses near our coasts. Based on their response to a recent event, it appears they are not.

We were disappointed the Senate ratified a treaty that contains language that could reduce our defensive weapons.

---

[101] Dr. Wood, Lowell, Statement, "*Threat Posed by Electromagnetic Pulse (EMP) to U.S. Military Systems and Civil Infrastructure*", U.S. House of Representative, Committee on National Security, Military Research and Development Subcommittee, Washington DC July 16 1997p 36

[102] Rep. Clarke, Yvette D., Opening Statement "*Securing the Modern Electric Grid from Physical and Cyber Attacks*" Subcommittee on Emerging Threats, Cybersecutiry and Science and Technology, Committee on Homeland Security, July 21, 2009

It is reasonable, especially at this time to prepare for an event and pray that it never happens. We need new leaders that place the protection of our nation against enemies at the top of their priorities. **God be with us.**

Appendix A: Other Survival Scenarios

In addition to an EMP initiated power grid failure there are other potential disasters. These may allow a longer period of communication and decision before evacuating. Based on the disaster type you should have an emergency contact plan.

Some disasters will not suddenly occur. There may be weeks of increasing risk before it becomes necessary to evacuate. A financial collapse would escalate over days and weeks providing some time for evacuation planning and notification. Financial collapse may not sound like a disaster, but read the history of Argentina's financial crisis and the chaos that followed last decade. A quarter of the population did not have enough money to buy food. Riots, arson and government collapse followed.

A nuclear war in a distant region of the world may escalate into a disaster at home over days or weeks. Any nuclear attack potential would suggest going to a stocked retreat location away from a major city, in advance of an attack. If a nuclear attack is imminent, find shelter as far from the target as possible and as far below ground as possible indoors, sealing doors and windows. Major cities would be obvious targets. Radiation injuries are related to the cumulative dose of radiation received. The following are some of the details in a U.S. Army manual:

Dose: 50-200 rad .- About six hours later the victim may have no symptoms or occasional headache. They expect no deaths in patients hospitalized.

Dose 200-500 rad.- Four to six hours after exposure individuals will experience headaches, weakness, nausea and vomiting. They will have difficulty with task for six to twenty hours. Less than 5% of the hospitalized victims at the low end of exposure will die.

Dose 500-1000 rad.- One to four hours after exposure severe and prolonged nausea and vomiting and diarrhea and fever in those in the higher exposure level. 50% will die and all within 45 days.

Dose 1000 rad or more- in less than one hour severe vomiting, diarrhea and weakness. All die within 30 days. Treatment of radiation exposure is washing to remove contaminants and symptomatic treatment. [103]

Chemical Weapons are designed to produce the following health issues; skin rash and blistering burns, pulmonary (breathing) problems, seizures, or acute hemolytic anemia.

Biological weapons known to be considered by enemies are; anthrax, cholera, legionnaires disease, plague, smallpox and typhus. Some remain virulent in the air from hours to days but on surfaces for a day to a year. An epidemic of illness will require isolation as the best defense. The best protection in a biologic attack is a pressured shelter using filtered air.

A biological weapon may be suspected if sudden illnesses are out of season, in a defined geography, excessive in numbers, and affect patients normally not susceptible. If ordinary treatments fail, it may also be a sign of biological warfare. If the epidemic is widespread when it is announced publicly, there is little time to leave. If it has a significant mortality or disables the victims, it will be best to stay isolated and at your home location than to be exposed in an evacuation or refugee camp. Remember

---

[103] U.S. Army, U.S. Army Special Forces Medical Handbook, March 1982, p 14-1

that clothing can transfer infections in dust particles too. Vaccinations should be kept up to date.

A computer virus attack could shut down the internet and information systems and affect commerce, banking and security. A customized computer virus could affect the electrical power grid, airline traffic control, gas line distribution, and other infrastructure systems that depend on computers. A dedicated attack by a foreign government could bring down many systems simultaneously. Military doctrines of China and Russia define information warfare as a spectrum ranging from computer viruses to nuclear EMP attack.[104]

Government take-over, assassinations, terrorist attacks and widespread riots should also activate the initial phases of your disaster plan.

---

[104] Dr. Pry, Peter Vincent , Statement, *"Terrorism and the EMP Threat to Homeland Security"*, U.S. Senate, Subcommittee on Terrorism, Technology and Homeland Security, March 8 2005

Appendix B: Survival WEB sites

(These are sites that we visited. You will find more in your search)

Communication Equipment Suppliers:

    www.icomamerica.com

    www.yaesu.com

    www.aesham.com

    www.arrl.org

    www.hamradio.com

    www.houstonamateurradiosupply.com

    www.radioshack.com

    www.universal-radio.com

EMP sites:

    www.empactamerica.org

    www.endtimesreport.com/EMP.html

    www.empcommission.org/docs

    http://archive.gao.gov/F0102/115200.pdf

    http://en.wikipedia.org/wiki/Electromagnetic_pulse

Government Sites:

    www.disasterassistance.gov

    www.fema.gov

    www.ready.gov

    www.whitehouse.gov/issues/homeland-security

Survival and Prepper (people or organizations that plan for survival) sites:

    www.americanpreppersnetwork.com

    www.prepper.org

    www.prepperbook.com

www.survivalblog.com

www.thesurvivalistblog.net

www.wilderness-survival.net

www.securityprousa.com

Sites for long term food storage:

www.beprepared.com

www.foodinsurance.com

www.ldscatalog.com

www.mountainhouse.com

www.nitro-pak.com

www.providentliving.com

www.quakekare.com

Survival Supplies:

www.2012supplies.com

www.cabelas.com

www.survival-goods.com

www.uscavalry.com

www.survivalsolutions.com

www.survivalunlimited.com

Alternative energy:

www.windstreampower.com

www.harborfreight.com

www.solar-cook.com

www.sunforceproducts.com

Hardware/Survival/Alternative Energy, custom consultation/orders:

Viola Emporium LLC, Viola WI email: violaemporium@mwt.net

Water filters (for pathogens)

     www.bigberkeywaterfilters.com

     www.xpackprepared.com

Military information:

     www.globalsecurity.org/military/library

Battery information:

     www.BatteryStuff.com

     www.windsun.com

     store.solar-electric.com

     www.all-battery.com

Appendix C: Checklist

This is a checklist for EMP attack preparation. The list starts with the easiest and least expensive items and progresses through a complete checklist.

Establish a plan:

Who will be in your survival group?   —

How will you communicate?   —

Where will you meet?   —

Where will your long term survival place be?   —

Transportation?   —

Who will declare the emergency?   —

What supplies will everyone bring?   —

Establish evaluation plan (if needed):

What vehicle(s)?   —

Establish alternate routes   —

Compute gas requirements   —

Buy siphon hose   —

Predetermine where traffic backups may occur and
how to circumvent   —

Start building caches of items you use normally:

Canned food   —

Boxed food (i.e. cereal or pasta)   —

Aluminum foil, plastic bags   —

Charcoal, propane   —

Dental supplies (toothpaste, floss, mouth wash)   —

Medication (prescription and over-the-counter)   —

Toilet paper   —

Save old clothing and shoes for trade or use   —

Keep cash on hand for emergencies   —

Save newspaper for starting fires   —

Save blankets, towels and rags   —

Store and identify a source for water:

Buy and fill a 35 gallon water tank   —

Prepare to drain water from your hot water heater   —

Buy plastic bags/containers to store water   —

Buy pool shock powder to make
chlorine for purification   —

Buy buckets to collect rain water   —

Identify sources of water   —

Purchase water filtration system/filters   —

Establish a sanitation plan:

Where will food be prepared?   —

How will you dispose of toilet waste?   —

How will you bathe with limited water?   ___

Build long term food supply:

#10 cans of wheat, oat, bean, rice   ___

#10 can of dried fruit   ___

Olive oil   ___

Buy and store survival supplies (see supplies chapter):

Communications   ___

Hardware store   ___

Camping store   ___

Internet   ___

Drug store   ___

Fabric store   ___

Grocery store   ___

Book store   ___

Gun shop   ___

Learn to use firearms:

Get gun license/permits   ___

Take gun safety classes   ___

Buy extra ammunition   ___

Practice shooting   ___

Install emergency power source:

Solar panels for electricity   —

Alternative heating source   —

Solar oven for cooking   —

Batteries, flashlights, radios

Research battery bank arrangements

    —

Two way Communications:

Buy portable CB/HAM radios

    —

Get amateur radio license   —

Establish emergency frequency/channels   —

Practice communication skills   —

Reinforce survival house

Upgrade to steel doors and strong locks   —

Precut plywood to fit windows   —

Add bulletproof steel armor by windows   —

Add 12 volts emergency lighting/alarms   —

Buy several large fire extinguishers   —

Appendix D: Survival Backpack

A survival backpack stored in you car will provide essential supplies as you travel to your survival home. The backpack should allow you to travel by foot if necessary. By having supplies pre-packed, you can leave immediately for your survival destination; before the roads become blocked. If the attack occurs while you are traveling you have supplies to get you to your destination. These are the supplies you should include:

MRE (Meal Ready-to-Eat) food or high calorie food bars

Water

Waterproof matches

Water filter and/or purification tablets

Flashlight/radio crank radio combo

Dust/pollution mask

First aid kit

Emergency all-in-one tool

Emergency blankets and sleeping bags (thermal reflective)

Bar soap

Toothbrush and toothpaste

Maps

Compass

Emergency rain ponchos

Tube tent

Facial tissues and Handkerchiefs

Disinfecting wipes

Heavy duty leather gloves

Disposable gloves

Notepad with pencil and sharpener

Spare prescription eye glasses

Necessary medication

Mace or gun for protection

Small shovel, stored separately in the car

Small saw, stored separately in the car

Appendix E: Recommended Reading and Survival Library

Auerbach, Paul S., <u>Medicine for the Outdoors,</u> Guilford, Ct, The Lyons Press, 2003

Bartmann, Dan and Dan Fink, <u>Homebrew Wind Power</u>, Masonville, CO, Buckville Publications, 2009

Black, David S. <u>Living off the Grid: a Simple Guide to Creating and Maintaining a Self-reliant Supply of Energy, Water, Shelter, and More.</u> New York: Skyhorse Pub., 2008.

Emergency Nurses Association, <u>The Family Emergency Handbook,</u> NY, NY, Playmore/Waldman, 2003

Foster, John S., Earl E. Gjelde, Graham, Dr. William R, et al, "*Critical National Infrastructures*", Report of the Commission to Assess the Threat to the United States from Electromagnetic Pulse (EMP) Attack, July 10, 2008, www.hsdl.org

Foster, John S., Earl E. Gjelde, Graham, Dr. William R, et al, *"Executive Summary"*, Report of the Commission to Assess the Threat to the United States from Electromagnetic Pulse (EMP), 2004, www.hsdl.org

Gibbons, Euell, Stalking The Wild Asparagus, David McKay Co Inc, 1964

Jaeger, Ellsworth, Wildwood Wisdom, Bolinas, CA, Shelter Publications, 1945

Major Miller, Colin R., USAF, *"Electromagnetic Pulse Threats in 2010*, Maxwell AFB, Al, Air War College, Center for Strategy and Technology, November 2005

Peterson, Lee Allen, A Field Guide to Edible Wild Plants, Peterson Field Guides, NY NY, Houghton Mifflin, 1977

Pitchford, Paul. Healing with Whole Foods: Asian Traditions and Modern Nutrition. Berkeley, CA: North Atlantic, 2002.

Robishaw, Sue. Homesteading Adventures: a Guide for Doers and Dreamers. Cooks, MI: ManyTracks, 1997.

Schaeffer, John, Solar Living Source Book, New Society Publishers Limited, Gabriola Island, BC, Canada 2008

Thayer, Samuel. The Forager's Harvest: a Guide to Identifying, Harvesting, and Preparing Edible Wild Plants. Ogema, WI: Forager's Harvest, 2006..

U. S. Army, Field Manual, Survival, 1970

U.S. Army, The Illustrated Guide to Edible Wild Plants, Guilford Ct, The Lyons Press, 2003

U.S. Army, Special Forces Medical Handbook. Beauport, Quebec: C.M.I.C., 1982.

U. S. House of Representatives, "Grid Reliability and Infrastructure Defense Act", Congressional Record, June 9, 2010, HR 5026

U.S. House of Representatives, *"Threat Posed by Electromagnetic Pulse (EMP) to U.S. Military Systems and Civil Infrastructure"*, Testimony, Committee on National Security, Military Research and Development Subcommittee, July 16 1997, www.commdocs.house.gov

U.S. House of Representatives, *"Threat Posed by Electromagnetic Pulse (EMP) Attack,* Committee on Armed Services, Washington DC, U.S. Government Printing Office, July 10 2008,

U.S. House of Representatives, *"Securing the Modern Electric Grid from Physical and Cyber Attacks"*, Committee on Homeland Security, Subcommittee on Emerging Threats, Cyber security, and Science and Technology, testimony, July 21, 2009 Washington DC, U.S. Government printing office, www.gpoaccess.gov/congress/index.html

U.S. House of Representatives, *"Electromagnetic Pulse Threats to U.S. Military and Civilian Infrastructure"*, Committee on Armed Services, Military Research and Development Subcommittee, October 7, 1999

U.S. Senate, *"Government Preparedness and Response to a Terrorist Attack Using Weapons of Mass Destruction*, Subcommittee on Terrorism and Homeland Security, Senate Judiciary Committee, August 4, 2010

U.S. Senate, *"Terrorism and the EMP Threat to Homeland Security"*, U.S. Senate Committee on the Judiciary, Subcommittee on Terrorism, Technology and Homeland Security", testimony, Mar 8 2005, U.S. Government Printing Office, Washington DC, www.hsdl.org

Weinstein, Raymond S., and Kenneth Alibek, <u>Biological and Chemical Terrorism, A Guide for Healthcare Providers and First Responders</u>, NY. NY Thieme Medical Publishers, Inc. 2003

Wolfgang, Larry D., (editor), <u>Now You're Talking!, All You Need to Get Your First Radio License,</u> 5th edition, Newington, Ct, The American Radio Relay League, Inc., (ARRL), 2003

Appendix F: Useful Weights and Measures

½ fluid ounce= 1 Tablespoon

1 Tablespoon=3 teaspoons

¼ cup =2 ounces=4 Tablespoons=6 teaspoons

¼ gallon=1 quart=2 pints=4 cups=32 fluid ounces

1 gallon=128 fluid ounces=3785 ml=4 quarts

1 teaspoon/per gallon= 65 ppm

1 pint = 2 cups

1quart = 4 cups

1gallon = 16 cups

1 cup = 8 ounces

1 tablespoon=15 grams

1 ounce= 30 grams

1 ounce= 30 ml

1 pound=454 grams

1 gram=.035274 ounces

1 millimeter=.03937 inches

1 meter=39.37 inches

1 teaspoon=60 "metric" drops=5ml

2 Tablespoons= 1 ounce

.01% salt solution in 8 ounces=144 grains of salt

Appendix G: An Inexpensive Solar Oven

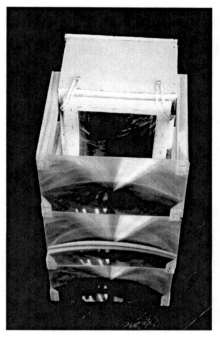

This picture shows an easy to build and inexpensive solar oven that we built. The cost is around $35 and can be made with simple tools.

We tested this design in mid December in Illinois winter, with a low sun and 25° temperature. The oven heated to 210°. It was sufficient heat to cook raw wheat in our trial. We added water to the wheat before cooking. The oven uses three fresnel lenses to direct the sun into a long loaf pan. Three pint sized canning jars fit into the long loaf pan inside the oven. We painted the outside of the pint canning jars black.

You could build one or two ovens for testing and personal use. Then buy the materials for ten or more ovens, in case you need them during the outage. During a survival situation you can use several for cooking and heating water. Extra ovens will be useful for trade.

The materials needed are:

A 16" x 4" x 4.5" long loaf pan (available for less than $10)

Three one pint wide mouth canning jars

Three 7-1/4" x 10-1/4" Fresnel lens ($2 at American Science and Surplus)

Half inch plywood

High temperature black paint

Nails and screws

Attic insulation

Plastic turkey oven bag.

Stick on half inch door insulation

Wood glue

To build the oven, cut a 8 ¼ " by 20" piece of plywood. Cut a rectangular hole in this piece that the long loaf pan will just fit into. Next, cut four pieces of plywood to form the sides of the box. (add the back later) The depth should be about seven inches. Build the box using wood glue and nails or screws. Screw the long loaf pan into place. Paint the pan, canning jars, and lids black. Add insulation around the long loaf pan and attach the back to the box. Attach the door insulation to the front around the pan. This will help seal the box cover.

Next, make a box cover out of plywood. Cut a hole in the cover so that the cover will go around the pan easily but fit snug to the door insulation. Cut two pieces of plastic from the oven bag that will fit on the front and back of the cover. Staple these into place. You can use two layers of glass if desired, but this will add to the cost.

The fresnel lenses need to be mounted about 6 ½ inches in front of the long loaf pan. This will create a two to three inch hot spot on the blackened canning jars. The middle lens should be centered. The upper and lower lenses need to be cut down to six inches width to keep the focus inside the box. Add four narrow wood pieces to each side of the box to support the fresnel lenses. Staple the lenses into place.

The cover is kept in place with four rubber bands. Add eight nails or screws to the corners of the box to hold the rubber bands in place.

In use, the oven will need to be tilted to focus the sun into the pan. We were able to do this by leaning the back against a milk carton (filled with water) and propping up the front. You could add some adjustment brackets if desired. The oven will need to be adjusted every half hour to follow the sun. Also, be careful you don't burn yourself on the fresnel lenses. These are strong magnifying lenses and can burn skin in seconds at the focal point (10 inches). Always use all three jars in the oven, since the design is based on heating the jars and not the back of the pan (which may get too hot without the jars).